IN SEARCH OF UNITY

In Search
of Unity

Edward Yarnold

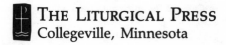
THE LITURGICAL PRESS
Collegeville, Minnesota

Original title: *In Search of Unity*. Copyright © St. Paul Publications, Slough, England, 1988. All rights reserved. This edition for the United States of America and Canada published by The Liturgical Press, Collegeville, Minnesota.

Printed in the United States of America.

1	2	3	4	5	6	7	8	9

Library of Congress Cataloging-in-Publication Data

Yarnold, Edward.
    In search of unity / Edward Yarnold.
       p. c.m
     ISBN 0-8146-1920-7
     1. Catholic Church—Relations—Anglican Communion. 2. Anglican
Communion—Relations—Catholic Church. 3. Catholic Church—Doctrines.
4. Anglican Communion—Doctrines. 5. Yarnold, Edward.
6. Anglican/Roman Catholic International Commission. I. Title.
BX5004.2.Y37   1990   89-77541
282—dc20   CIP

Contents

INTRODUCTION

This little book on ecumenism has at least two limitations. The first is that in writing it I have confined myself largely to my experience as a member of the Anglican-Roman Catholic International Commission since its inception in 1970. I have therefore had little to say about the achievements of the many other bilateral discussions which have been proceeding fruitfully over the same years, such as the Roman Catholic-Methodist conversations, which have produced four common declarations, or the Roman Catholic-Orthodox dialogue, which has produced two. Nor have I given much space to the strikingly successful work of the Faith and Order Commission, which involves all the major Christian Churches. It is not until the final chapter that I have devoted even brief attention to these wider horizons.

Some readers may judge that the present work suffers from a second limitation, namely, that its approach is not sufficiently radical. I am aware of the prophetical ecumenical path mapped out by Karl Rahner, who believed that the reunion of the Churches is not only necessary but possible *already*.[1] A "realistic" consensus in faith, he believed, could be achieved without

1. See, for example, K. Rahner and H. Fries, *Unity of the Church: an Actual Possibility*, Philadelphia, 1985. The position held by these two authors has been criticized by A. Dulles, *The Reshaping of Catholicism: Current Challenges in the Theology of the Church*, San Francisco, 1988, 233–36.

the need for further doctrinal discussions. Each of the Churches which accept the traditional creeds of the first centuries could not agree not to reject whatever is held as a binding dogma in any of the other Churches; more detailed agreement could be worked out in the future. What I have written in chapters 2 and 5 on the ecumenical virtues of hope and trust perhaps reveals that Rahner's strategy has exerted some influence on my thought. Nevertheless, I have not entered into an explicit discussion of this strategy, and for a simple reason. Ecumenism, like politics, is the art of the possible. I did not wish to weaken the thrust of such a short book as this by proposing solutions which, as far as human calculations go, can have no hope of success at the present time. I therefore have adopted a much more traditional approach, which is based on the search first for agreement in faith, and then, at every stage, for the appropriated realization of that agreement in terms of practical relations between the Churches.

In the final chapter I have written, factually, I hope, rather than with recrimination or pessimism, that in some ways the gap between Canterbury and Rome is wider now than it was when ARCIC began its work in 1970. In writing this, I have concentrated on the ways in which the Anglican Communion has been moving further away from Rome. Roman Catholics need however to realize that to many Anglicans the reverse is at least equally true. For them, it is Rome that has been moving away from Anglicanism. Whereas the concept of collegiality developed at Vatican II gave many Anglicans hope that they could accept a papacy which functioned within collegial checks and balances, Rome's reassertion of central authority in recent years makes some wonder whether their hopes were illusory.

Relations between the two Churches are in a state of crisis, in the word's strict sense of a point of decision. At such a time it is vital that the two Churches should not indulge in mutual accusations of shifting goal-posts, but should see what they can do to help one another. Ecumenism involves bearing one another's burdens. Roman Catholics, for example, should try to feel what it is about the papacy which other Churches find unacceptable and regard it as a duty to change what can be changed and to help the other Churches to see the Christian value in what must not be changed. Anglicans should not rebuke Roman Catholics for refusing to recognize their orders but should try to appreciate why objections are made and what can be done either to dispel them or to meet them.

By the time readers have reached the end of this book, they may be left with the feeling that the prospects for reunion are bleak. I have come to believe that the road to unity, even between two Churches which have so much in common as the Roman Catholic and the Anglican, is much harder to map than I and many others imagined in our post-Vatican II ecumenical optimism. Nevertheless, as Pope John Paul II stated on the day when he was installed as pope, "The commitment of the Catholic Church to the ecumenical movement . . . is irreversible."

We are confident that he who began this work among us will give us abundantly the strength to persevere and carry it out successfully.[2]

We need to be clear-sighted in recognizing the facts if we wish to remedy them.

Some sections of this book have appeared at greater length elsewhere. Parts of Chapters 1 and 3 follow closely my pamphlet *The Church and the Churches*, CTS, London 1984. The discussion of the doctrine of the Blessed Virgin Mary is a shorter version of my article "Mary and ARCIC," *The Month*, February 1989. I am grateful to the publishers for permission to use this material.

I would like to thank most warmly those friends who read all or part of this work in draft and made valuable suggestions: my fellow Jesuits, Robert Murray and Norman Tanner; my ARCIC colleagues, Mary Tanner and Christopher Hill; and for his valuable reflections on Rahner, to my colleague at this Hall, Richard Lennan.

Campion Hall
Oxford
April 1989

2. *TAIE*, 153–54.

Chapter 1

THE PARADOX:
ONE BUT DIVIDED

Sixteen hundred years ago the First Council of Constantinople added to the Nicene Creed the affirmation: "We believe . . . in one, holy, catholic, and apostolic Church." In these words every Sunday at Mass Christians profess their acceptance of that statement. Unity is one of the "marks" of the Church, a quality which is essential to the very existence of the Church, a characteristic by which we can tell the true Church from the false. And yet, as is only too evident, Christians are not united. Has the Church lost one of its essential qualities?

Two Differing Views About Unity

A cynical bishop is reported to have said, "I believe in the one, holy, catholic, and apostolic Church, and regret that it does not exist." His solution to the problem of the difference between the Church one believes in and the Church as it actually is, is simple and soothing: the unity of the Church is a promise which will be fulfilled only in heaven, an ideal which is a challenge to us but which we shall never do more than approach. Such a view, however, would rob ecumenism of its chief motive power. The ecumenist would be working for an end which he knew would never be fulfilled.

Some Christians account for the inconsistency between their profession of faith in unity and actual divisions in another way. The unity which is an essential quality of the Church is for them not a unity among organized Christian bodies, but an internal unity of Christians based on faith, love, and obedience to the Word of God. This point was brought home to me in the mid-sixties at two of the first ecumenical meetings at which I took part as a speaker. In those days, which followed shortly after Vatican II, one of the most popular ways of implementing the Council's call to unity was to bring together on a single platform a number of speakers from different Churches to explain their understanding of ecumenism. On each of these two occasions, someone felt obliged to say that he believed the ecumenical movement to be misguided because it implied that the visible, structural aspect of the Church was important. On the contrary, it was said, the only unity that mattered was that which existed between true Christians who "loved the Lord Jesus in their hearts."

The point these speakers were making was not the comfortable one that all the Churches are already united because their members all love the Lord. Their message was more critical and bleak. As they saw it, the Churches had fallen into the error of attributing an absolute value to man-made things like Church organization. True unity was that which united the relatively few among the members of any Church who refused to absolutize externals, and were at one, whatever their denomination, in their fidelity to Jesus Christ.

The Catholic View of Ecumenism

The Catholic understanding of ecumenism is opposed to both these views. (1) Against the cynics and the unhopeful, it maintains that the unity of the Church is not something which will come about only in heaven but a gift which has already been given to Christ's followers. (2) Against those who limit unity to an internal quality of faith and love, the Catholic Church teaches that the unity Christ gives is not an invisible bond uniting a small élite of true disciples; it is a visible unity which joins Churches as well as individuals.

Church's Unity Is Essential Gift

The Vatican II Decree on Ecumenism spoke of "the unity of the one and only Church" as a gift "which Christ bestowed on his Church from the beginning" (n. 4). Pope John Paul II reflected that view when he told Church leaders in Germany: "The unity of the Church undeniably belongs to her essence." The same belief is reflected in the Final Report of the Anglican-Roman Catholic International Commission (ARCIC): "Unity is of the essence of the Church" (Introduction n. 9).

The Church's inalienable unity is the consequence of its indefectibility. This indefectibility means that despite the weakness and sin of its members the power of the Holy Spirit will keep the Church in being and keep it true to its fundamental nature. Christ will fulfill his promise that the gates of hell will not prevail against his Church (Matt 16:18). Now, an essential aspect of the Church's nature is unity. As Pope John Paul II reminded the members of ARCIC when he received them in audience at Castel Gandolfo in 1980, "unity is a gift of our Lord and Savior, the founder of the Church. Although it was marred by the sin of men, it was never entirely lost." It follows that Jesus' final prayer that "they may all be one" (John 17:21) has its fulfillment here and now.

Jesus went on to pray that "they may become perfectly one" (John 17:23). The complete fulfillment of that prayer has never yet come about since the time of St. Paul when the Church was already split by jealousies and disagreements. It is only in heaven that our unity will be "perfect," but the initial gift of fundamental unity is already one of the "first fruits of the Spirit" (cf. Rom 8:23).

Unity Must Be Visible

This unity with which Christ endowed his Church, and which already exists, though imperfectly, must be visible. To quote the Introduction to the Final Report again: "Since the Church is visible its unity also must be visible" (n. 9). The fourth chapter of the Epistle to the Ephesians lists some of the aspects of this unity. It is indeed an internal unity of those knit together as organs sharing the common life of Christ's body—a unity of those who share one hope, one faith, one Spirit, one Lord, one God and Father. But it is also to be expressed outwardly in "a life worthy of the calling to which you have been called" (4.1), a life characterized by lowliness, meekness, patience, forbearance, and peace. This outward expression of interior unity includes the social forms or structures of the Church: "one baptism" and "one body"—a body that is not only the Eucharistic body which makes Christians one but also the social body of the Church's life in which Christians are endowed with a diversity of ministerial gifts, as apostles, prophets, evangelists, pastors, teachers, "to equip the saints for the work of ministry, for building up the body of Christ" (4.12).

This already existing unity of the Church can be described as "communion," sharing, participation; to express this range of meaning, modern writers sometimes use the New Testament Greek term *koinonia*. The word can be translated as "fellowship," as in St. John's statement of his reason for writing his first epistle: "so that you may have fellowship with us, and our fellowship is with the Father and with his Son Jesus Christ" (1 John 1:3). The Introduction to ARCIC I's Final Report is for the most part a description of the Church in terms of *koinonia*. This *koinonia* is, at its deepest level, "union with God in Christ Jesus through the Spirit"; a sharing in the Spirit of God the Son who shared our nature; a sharing in a common life with all other members of that body who together receive the Body in its Eucharistic form which we call holy communion, holy "sharing" (Intro. 56).

The Vatican II Decree on Ecumenism goes further, stating that "the unity, in the Trinity of Persons, of one God, the Father, and the Son in the Holy Spirit" is not only the "highest source" but also the "exemplar" of the unity of the Church (n. 2). This affirmation is doubtless inspired by Jesus' prayer to his Father that his followers "may all be one; even as thou, Father, art in me, and I am in thee" (John 17:21). There is, however, a danger that the comparison our Lord expresses may be taken too far. The unity that is proper to the Church is a unity of separate beings.

In our communion with one another and with God we do not cease to be individual human beings, endowed with individual minds and wills. This is not the same kind of unity in diversity as that which belongs to the three Persons of the Trinity. If the Father, the Son, and the Holy Spirit were persons in the same sense as we are persons, each endowed with his own mind and will, there would be three Gods, however closely they were united in love.

Jesus, the Example of Unity

Jesus' words therefore call for a different interpretation. The unity of his followers is not to be compared directly with the unity of the eternal Father, Son, and Spirit but with the unity that exists between the incarnate Jesus Christ and his heavenly Father. Jesus' words quoted above continue: "that they may be one even as we are one, I in them and thou in me" (John 17:22-23). Jesus' food was to do his Father's will (John 4:34). He had the most intimate knowledge of his Father (Matt 11:27); he did nothing of his own accord but only what he saw his Father doing (John 5:19). It is Jesus' intimate knowledge of his Father, his loving submission to him, and the Father's reciprocal love for Jesus, which are held out to us as the model for the unity of Christians.

Jesus' prayer for the unity of his followers contains also other forms of guidance and inspiration for Christians seeking reunion. He prays that his followers may be one "so that the world may believe that thou [Father] hast sent me" (John 17:21). In the next chapter we shall consider what this prayer has to tell us about the missionary nature of ecumenism. The fundamental reason for seeking Christian unity is the conviction that a divided Christianity makes not only the Church but Christ himself less credible. For the time being our concern is with another implication of Christ's words: if the unity of his followers is to be evidence on his behalf, both his followers and their unity must be recognizable. If the identity of Christ's true followers and their unity were an internal fact known only to himself, it would be useless as evidence.

In Chapter 4, we shall give further consideration to the visible nature of the unity of Christians and ask what this recognizable unity consists of. For the present we return to the great ecumenical paradox: unity—and visible unity at that—is an essential characteristic of Christ's Church, yet the Church is divided.

The Paradox of Disunity

This was a paradox which official Roman Catholic thinking on Church unity failed to recognize until Vatican II. The First Vatican Council, which was prevented from completing its work by the threat of war in 1870, got as far as producing a draft decree on the Church, in which the Church is defined as "the multitude . . . which is governed by our Lord and Saviour himself through his vicar on earth and the other pastors [bishops]." In other words, the Church was said to consist only of those Christians who are in communion with the Pope. The visible unity of the Church is safe-guarded, but only at the cost of excluding all who are not Roman Catholics.

Although the draft never acquired official status, this attitude to Christians outside the Roman Catholic Church continued to prevail. Pope Pius XII, in an encyclical written in 1943, explained that the "true Church," which is called the Mystical Body of Jesus Christ, is "the Holy, Catholic, Apostolic, Roman Church" (*Mystici Corporis*, n. 13). One cannot "adhere to Christ as Head of the Church without loyal allegiance to his Vicar on earth" (n. 39). The Pope did, however, soften this teaching by allowing for those who, though not members of the Roman Catholic Church, are "related to the Mystical Body of the Redeemer by some unconscious yearning and desire" (n. 102). Nevertheless, it is evidently Pius XII's view that such people of good faith are not members of Christ's Church nor of his Body, either as individuals or as members of their particular denominations. He reiterated this teaching in his encylical *Humani Generis* of 1950, in which he wrote that it was "a doctrine based on revealed truth" that "the Mystical Body of Christ and the Catholic Church in communion with Rome are one and the same thing" (n. 27).

Vatican II Drafts on Church Unity

When the Second Vatican Council returned to the same theme, the earliest drafts of what was to become the Dogmatic Constitution *Lumen Gentium*—on the Church—continued to regard the Church of Christ and the Roman Catholic Church as coextensive. The first of these drafts, produced by the Preparatory Commission in November 1962, stated that there is only one true Church of Jesus Christ, namely that which we proclaim in the Creed as one, holy, catholic, and apostolic and which the Savior won for himself on the cross, joined to himself as the body to the head and the bride to the bridegroom, and after his resurrection entrusted to St. Peter and his successors, the Bishops of Rome, for them to govern; consequently, it alone has the right to be called the Roman Catholic Church (n. 7).

A second draft proposed several changes in this passage. Among them was the modification of the last clause so that it now made the identity between Christ's Church and the Roman Catholic Church even more explicit:

> Therefore this heavenly Church, animated, united, and sanctified by the Holy Spirit, is the community of grace and love organically established on earth as a society, namely, the Catholic Church which is Roman.

In the succeeding months several national groups of bishops put forward other modifications of the text. Among these drafts was one proposed by some French bishops and theologians, which stated that the visible Church is made up of many elements which non-Catholic Christians can share so as to be joined to the Church "in Christ's own way" (*modo a Christo stabilito*). Nevertheless, the visible Church itself "is only found where every one of these means of grace is found, namely, in the Roman Catholic Church" (III; II.6). In other words, the French bishops still asserted the identity between Christ's Church and the Roman Catholic Church but now give a reason for that assertion, namely, that it is only in the Roman Catholic Church that all the means of salvation are to be found.

A revised draft of the whole document was circulated in the middle of 1963. The passage we have been considering now appeared in a developed form of the second version of the previous November:

> Accordingly, this Church [the one Church of Christ], which is the true Mother and Mistress of us all, established and disposed in this world as a society, is the Catholic Church directed by the Bishop of Rome and the bishops in communion with him, even though outside its total structure there can be found a number (*plura*) of elements of sanctification which, belonging as they do to the Catholic Church, are forces impelling towards catholic unity (n. 7).

Thus the Church of Christ is still said to be identical with the Roman Catholic Church though the reason suggested by the French bishops is not reproduced. However, this draft differs from all previous versions in its assertion that the elements of sanctification present in other Churches "impel" them towards unity with the Roman Catholic Church.

In the following years, the Council's Doctrinal Commission proposed further modifications to the text. In addition to various minor changes in the passage under examination, now numbered section 8, it was recommended that, instead of stating that the one Church of Christ is the Catholic Church directed by the Bishop of Rome, the document should say that Christ's Church "subsists" in that Church; such a turn of phrase would be, it was explained, more consistent with the affirmation that elements of the Church exist outside the Roman Catholic Church.

In this form the draft was submitted to the members of the Council for comment. Four further modifications were proposed. Nineteen Fathers proposed the formula "subsists in its integrity to the Catholic Church." Twenty-five wished to say that Christ's Church "subsists by divine law" in the Catholic Church. One proposed to replace the word "subsists" by "consists." Thirteen wished to return to the assertion that the Church of Christ is the Catholic Church governed by the Pope. Noting that "two tendencies are evident, one for somewhat enlarging the sense of the text, the other for restricting it," the Doctrinal Commission judged that none of these alterations was necessary.

The Constitution's Final Definition of the Church

Consequently, the form of words which entered into the final version of the Dogmatic Constitution was as follows:

> This Church [of Christ], established and disposed in this world as a society, subsists in the Catholic Church, governed by the successor of Peter and the bishops in communion with him, even though there are found outside its structure a number of elements of sanctification and truth which, as gifts belonging to the Church of Christ, are forces impelling towards catholic unity.

In substituting the phrase "subsists in" for the original "is," it is evident that the Council was intending to express a relationship between Christ's Church and non-Christians which would not contradict the unique position of the Roman Catholic Church. The Doctrinal Commission rejected any form of words which might be taken to imply that Christ's Church subsists in other Churches, even in an incomplete way. Nevertheless, they rejected equally any phrase which excluded other Churches from Christ's Church altogether.

However, while the reasons for the choice of the term "subsists" are clear, the Council Fathers neglected to give any definition of the word and so bequeathed to commentators a legacy of obscurity. One possible interpretation of the clause would be that the Roman Catholic Church, whatever its shortcomings, is the embodiment in history of the Church Christ founded while other Churches are simply collections of individuals in whom God's grace is at work. It would be as if one said that private teaching institutions in a university city perform a useful educational service but are not part of the University and therefore cannot award degrees.

Roman Catholic Attitude Toward Orthodox Churches

Cardinal Jan Willebrands, the President of the Vatican Secretariat for Christian Unity, has argued convincingly that this would be a false interpretation of the mind of the Council. This is particularly evident in the Roman Catholic attitude to the Orthodox Churches. These are regarded as authentic Churches, though separated from the Roman Catholic Church. The one Church of Christ is divided. The Formula of Union devised by the Council of Florence, which in 1439 briefly healed the breach between the Roman Catholic and the Orthodox Churches, spoke of the removal of "the wall which separated the Western and Eastern Church," rather than of the return of the Orthodox to the true Church of Christ in the Roman Catholic Church. What the Council said about the subsistence of Christ's Church in the Roman Catholic Church must be interpreted in the light of this traditional recognition of the Orthodox Churches.

Importance of Other Churches Also

It is true that Rome accords to the Orthodox a unique place among the Churches from which it is separated. Nevertheless, another of the Vatican II documents, the Decree on Ecumenism, shows that the Council believes it is true of other Churches, too, that they "have been by no means deprived of significance and importance in the mystery of salvation." They are "means of salvation" (n. 3). In other words, it is these bodies, as bodies, which God has endowed with the "elements of sanctification and truth" which belong to Christ's Church. God's grace works among Christians who are not Roman Catholics, not as so many individuals but through their membership in their own Churches. If the elements of the Church are present in these communities, as communities, they must themselves be part of Christ's Church.

Unique Position of the Roman Catholic Church

What then constitutes the unique position of the Roman Catholic Church which the term "subsists" implies? What is lacking to those who are not Roman Catholics, which makes the Decree on Ecumenism state that our separated brethren, whether considered as individuals or as communities and Churches, are not blessed with that unity which Jesus Christ wished to bestow

(n. 3); and that it is through Christ's [Roman] Catholic Church alone, which is the universal help towards salvation, that the fullness of the means of salvation can be obtained (n. 3)?

The answer of Vatican II is that to be "fully incorporated" into Christ's Church means to "accept all the means of salvation given to the Church together with her entire organization" (*Lumen Gentium*, n. 14). Necessarily included among these means of salvation which are lacking to Christians who are not Roman Catholics is communion with the Pope and integration with "the visible structure of the Church of Christ, who rules her through the Supreme Pontiff and the bishops." Nevertheless, the conclusion to be drawn is not that those Churches which are not in communion with the Bishop of Rome are not incorporated in Christ's Church at all but rather that they are incorporated less than "fully." To be incorporated into Christ's Church admits of degrees.

The Papacy as a Sign of Communion

It is Catholic teaching that the papacy has arisen in the Church as a result of divine guidance and that the Church is not free to dispense with it. Why the primacy of the Bishop of Rome is of such importance among the elements of sanctification and truth with which the Church is endowed will be discussed in a later chapter. For the time being we may say that, if the Church exists for the communion of its members with God and with one another, it needs the papacy as the sign and instrument of this communion. To be separated from communion with the Pope is therefore to be lacking an essential element of the Church.

We began this chapter by asking how Christ's Church can be both inalienably one and also divided. We can now present the outline of an answer which will be filled out in subsequent chapters. The gifts of sanctification and truth which belong to all Christian bodies establish the Church in its unity. But the Church is divided because there is one of these gifts which, by definition, belongs only to the Roman Catholic Church, namely, communion with the Bishop of Rome.

Chapter 2

THE SPIRIT OF ECUMENISM

Having served on the Anglican-Roman Catholic International Commission since 1970, I have enjoyed traveling to many parts of the world for our annual meetings. After one of our sessions in Venice, which has been our most frequent meeting place, the *Catholic Herald* carried a cartoon of a party of merry ecumenists in a gondola enjoying themselves hugely, one of whom is expressing the hope that the search for reunion will prove a long process. The cartoon was actually based on a true incident which took place after the Patriarch of Venice (later Pope John Paul I whose papacy was sadly so brief) had entertained the Commission at dinner in his palazzo—though the reader should know that the gondola was a figment of the artist's imagination and the remark quoted was made by a consultant and not by a member of the Commission itself.

I mention this story simply in order to lead up to the statement that, in return for the privileged experience of working on the Commission, I feel under an obligation to accept as many as possible of the invitations I receive to go around giving talks on ARCIC. The most frequent question put to me by the audiences I address is: ''How hopeful are you that reunion between Anglicans and Roman Catholics will ever be achieved?'' I shall not give my full answer to that question here; perhaps the reader after reading this book will be able to reconstruct it. But one of the things I like to say is that my personal hopes have nothing to do with the matter. I do what I can to help the two Churches to reunite, not because I am optimistic of success but because it is my duty.

The Duty to Pursue Unity

It is a duty for several reasons. The least important but not wholly negligible reason is the administrative advantage of unity. Like commercial enterprises, Churches can make things easier for themselves by achieving a merger. Duplication of buildings and of staff can be avoided. Shortages of clergy can thus be overcome and clerical training improved. At a less material level, a united Christian voice is more likely to command the respect of secular authorities than a divided one. At the time of the historic meeting between the Archbishop of Canterbury (Dr. Michael Ramsey) and Pope Paul VI in 1966, a cartoonist—whether it was the same cartoonist I cannot recall—showed the two leaders embracing, while at the side one cleric said to another: "What Marx has joined together let no man put asunder."

However, the search for Christian unity is based on more important foundations. The basic reason is that Jesus Christ prayed for the unity of his followers in his final prayer which we considered in the first chapter:

> I do not pray for these only, but also for those who believe in me through their word, that they may all be one; even as thou, Father, art in me, and I in thee, that they also may be in us, so that the world may believe that thou hast sent me (John 17:20-21).

We have already concluded that this prayer of Jesus has its fulfillment even in this life because unity is an essential property of the Church. Jesus' prayer was heard and granted. Nevertheless, as we shall see in Chapter 4, unity admits of degrees. We must not, then, rest content with the limited degree of unity which Christians enjoy now. What Jesus prayed for, we, as his followers, are obliged to work for, namely, that we may become "perfectly one" (John 17:23). It is for this reason that the Second Vatican Council in its Decree on Ecumenism exhorts . . . all the Catholic faithful to recognize the signs of the times and to take an active and intelligent part in the work of ecumenism (n. 4).

The Search for Unity Is Demanded by the Spirit

In the same vein recent popes have stated that the search for unity among Christians is, in the present age, "the foremost demand of the Spirit," that it is required of us by obedience to God's word, that it is one of the first duties of Christians. We cannot be true Catholics, we cannot be true Christians, without being dedicated to the search for the full, visible, and corporate expression of the unity of Christ's followers.

However, it is not only a sense of duty which should prompt us to the pursuit of unity; Christians who wish to imitate Christ will share his heart's desire that his followers should be one. For Jesus, however, Christian unity was not only an end in itself; he prayed that the unity of his followers would lead unbelievers to faith in him. We should be one, he prayed, "so that the world may believe that thou hast sent me" (John 17:21). The implications of this prayer are awesome.

At an earlier point in St. John's account of the Last Supper, Jesus tells his disciples: "A new commandment I give to you, that you love one another; even as I have loved you, that you also love one another. By this all men will know that you are my disciples, if you have love for one another" (13:34-35).

Self-sacrifice, the Mark of a Christian

The demand this new commandment makes is vast enough. Jesus, "having loved his own who were in the world, . . . loved them to the end" (John 13:1). He loved them to the end of his life but also to the limit of self-sacrifice: "Greater love has no man than this, that a man lay down his life for his friends" (John 15:13). Jesus' words imply that Christians in their love for one another must be prepared to go to the same lengths. If they are not capable of such generosity, they are no disciples of his. This is such an essential characteristic of Christians that people can judge from its presence or absence whether we are true followers of his or not.

But the responsibility which Jesus' later saying lays upon us is even more vast. His prayer clearly implies that Christians carry the responsibility of proving by their unity in love not only the truth about themselves, "men will know that you are my disciples," but the truth about Jesus himself, "that the world may believe that thou hast sent me." Jesus has such confidence in the power of the Holy Spirit uniting his disciples in love for one another that, so to speak, he lays his own reputation on the line. But to put it that way is to trivialize the truth. Jesus was never concerned with his reputation for its own sake. The keynote of his life is the faithful performance of his Father's will (John 4:34). It is for the sake of his Father that he wants it to be known that the Father has sent him but also for the sake of the human beings whom he came to save and to whom he reveals the saving and life-giving truth: "This is eternal life, that they may know thee the only true God, and Jesus Christ whom thou has sent" (John 17:3). Christians are laden with the responsibility of proving by their unity the truth that meant so much to Jesus, namely, that the Father had sent him.

I often ask myself whether this really is the way people judge the truth of Christianity and therefore the truth about Christ. Would average Western agnostics be more inclined to become Christians if they saw the Churches reunited? It is hard to say. But I have noticed that agnostic journalists, at least, do not seem to want the Churches to be united and are prone to express something like contempt for the Churches' search for doctrinal agreement. Perhaps they feel less secure at the prospect of a genuinely united Christianity. Or is it simply that unity is less newsworthy than rivalry?

The Effect of Disunity

However that may be, the sophisticated Western attitude to Christian divisions is not the only one. I remember well hearing a retired Anglican missionary bishop in Jerusalem, in the course of a sermon delivered at the beginning of Church Unity Week, telling the congregation of a sad experience he had had. A tribe had determined to embrace Christianity but became so confused, or perhaps repelled, at the need to choose between several rival Churches all competing for the tribe's allegiance that they remained in their original religion. It was presumably some such danger which another Anglican bishop had in mind when he said at the 1988 Lambeth Conference that in Papua, New Guinea, unity between Anglicans and Roman Catholics was a missionary priority.

These various motives for ecumenism are well summed up in the opening paragraph of the Vatican II Decree on Ecumenism:

> Such division openly contradicts the will of Christ, scandalizes the world, and damages that most holy cause, the preaching of the Gospel to every creature.

Reconciliation

Pope John Paul II has put forward another reason for the Christian obligation to seek unity. The subject of the Good News which Jesus Christ entrusted to the Church is reconciliation: the reconciliation of human beings to God, "God was in Christ reconciling the world to himself" (2 Cor 5:19), but also the reconciliation of human beings one with another. It is not only concerning the relations between Jews and Gentiles that it can be said of Christ that

> he is our peace, who has made us both one, and has broken down the dividing wall of hostility . . . that he might create in himself one new man in place of the two, so making peace, and might reconcile us both to God in one body through the cross, thereby bringing the hostility to an end (Eph 2:14-16).

But the Church cannot proclaim this message of reconciliation which God has entrusted to it with any plausibility as long as Christians are unable to be reconciled among themselves. Once again, we see that the service the Church is called to fulfill for humankind is weakened by Christian divisions. Once again we see those divisions standing in the way of God's loving purposes.

There is one more reason why Christians should recognize the duty to work for Christian unity. We should feel love and respect for our fellow Christians in other Churches so strongly that to be separated from them should arouse in us a sense of pain and loss. Some Christians feel the pain of separation most acutely when they attend the Eucharist with members of another Church, but are unable to join them in receiving the Lord's Body and Blood which are the source and highest symbol of Christian unity. We shall return to the subject of Eucharistic sharing in Chapter 4. Our point for now is that, by reaction, communion can be shared by separated Christians too easily, so that the pain of division is never felt and that the most powerful stimulus for the search after real unity is lost.

Sin of Separation

There is a last reason why ecumenism is an essential Christian duty: the separation of Christian Churches is a sinful situation. The Decree on Ecumenism speaks explicitly of "the sin of separation" (n. 3):

> St. John has testified: "If we say we have not sinned, we make him a liar, and his word is not in us" (1 John 1:10). This holds good for sins against unity. Thus, in humble prayer we beg pardon of God and of our separated brethren, just as we forgive them that offend us (n. 7).

Indeed, schism has traditionally been regarded as one of the most serious sins. Although few theologians would now subscribe to the literal sense of St. Cyprian's dictum, "No salvation outside the Church," at least it is a reminder of the seriousness of the sin of schism. Schism is sinful in two senses. First, schisms came about originally as the result of the sins of individuals and groups; secondly, we today, although we were not responsible for the creation of the various schisms centuries ago, can easily contribute to the continuation of the schisms in our own time. These two levels of sin against the unity of the Church we might call respectively ecumenical original and actual sins.

Shared Blame

The Decree on Ecumenism confesses that Catholics shared the original sin. After the ''certain rifts'' which are evident even in the Church of the apostolic age, such as those in the Corinthian Church which St. Paul censures (1 Cor 11:8-19), the Council refers to ''much more serious dissensions'' when

> large communities became separated from full communion with the Catholic Church for which, often enough, men of both sides were to blame (n. 3).

To put the point in another way, in the Roman Catholic understanding of the Church, the act of voluntarily going into schism can never be justified and is always, objectively at least, sinful. Whatever the defects of the Roman Catholic Church may be in any time or place, one's duty is to stay within it and seek to correct it; if one gets excommunicated for one's protest, that is something which loyal Catholic reformers have had to bear. Mary Ward, for example, the holy foundress of the Institute of the Blessed Virgin Mary, was excommunicated for her original vision of religious life for women; she was subsequently vindicated and the cause of her beatification is proceeding. Nevertheless, although it cannot be right in itself—or objectively—to cut oneself off from the Roman Catholic Church, doubtless many people who have voluntarily gone into schism have done so because they believed no other course was open to them: ''I can no other,'' as Luther affirmed. Such people would be following their conscience and therefore not choosing subjectively to commit sin. However, whether there was subjective sin on the part of the one leaving the Catholic Church or not, there will often have been sin on the Catholic side in creating or tolerating the conditions which make continuance in that Church insupportable for the reforming spirit. How much of the responsibility for the sixteenth-century schism rests on the shoulders of Catholic authorities who created or failed to correct scandals, such as the worldliness of the papacy and the abuse of the system of indulgence which made many feel that it was morally imperative to cut themselves off from such a Church?

Hindrances to Healing Schism

However, as the Decree on Ecumenism points out, "one cannot charge with the sin of separation those who at present are born into these [non-Catholic] communities" (n. 3). Nor are twentieth-century Catholics to blame for the abuses which occasioned the breach of four hundred and fifty years ago. In other words, the original sins of schism are not imputable to us today. But we cannot so easily acquit ourselves of the other level of ecumenical sin which I have called ecumenical actual sin. Our words, actions, and attitudes can hinder the healing of schisms and so contribute to their continuance. We have in our age become more sensitive to the evil of racism, recognizing the subtle but corrosive poison of the sneer and the cheap ethnic joke as well as more blatant social and economic injustices. We need to develop the same sensitivity in regard to ecumenism.

It is not difficult to construct an ecumenical examination of conscience. Do I make fun of other Churches in ways in which I would not make fun of my own? Do I express and encourage prejudices? Am I content with my ignorant preconceptions of other Churches, or do I do what I can to correct them? Am I jealous of the success of other Churches? Do I recognize that their members are no less dear to our Lord than my correligionists are? Do I esteem and love them as fellow disciples? Do I long to be reunited with them in one Church, to share with them at one altar? Apart from harmful words and thoughts, am I guilty of ecumenical sins of omission? Do I miss opportunities of welcoming members of other Churches? Do I ever talk to them about faith or pray with them?

Ecumenical Virtues

In contrast with the ecumenical sins we have been considering, one can also consider the ecumenical virtues. The Decree on Ecumenism reminds us that the search for unity requires "spiritual ecumenism" (n. 8):

> There can be no ecumenism worthy of the name without interior conversion. For it is from newness of attitudes of mind, from self-

denial and unstinted love, that desires of unity take their rise and develop in a mature way. . . . The faithful should remember that they promote union among Christians better, that indeed they live it better, when they try to live holier lives according to the Gospel. For the closer their union with the Father, the Word and the Spirit, the more deeply and easily will they be able to grow in mutual brotherly love (n. 7).

Some of the ecumenical virtues we have already considered, such as love and esteem of other Christians and penitence for one's own ecumenical sins and for the ecumenical original sins of one's own Church. Another ecumenical virtue is open-mindedness. One needs to be able to get inside the skin of other Christians so as to experience the way they think and pray; and to do all this with the desire to find there the truth which one can acknowledge and share rather than error which one must reject and try to refute.

Ecumenical Virtue of Hope

To do this requires the ecumenical virtue of hope. We can trust in the success of the search for unity not on the evidence of the progress which has been achieved, though we must never allow weariness to blind us to the great gains that have been made, but rather because hope gives us confidence. Hope requires us to trust that grace will have its way, not only in heaven, but here below. We have Christ's promise that the gates of hell will not prevail against his Church (Matt 16:18). Moreover, we may be confident that, long before the ecumenical movement was heard of, God was at work in the Churches drawing them together. Whatever the motives, good and bad, which contributed to the original separation of Churches, since then, in their sincere attempts to be faithful to God's word and the promptings of the Holy Spirit, Christians have certainly been growing closer to each other. Consequently, although historical scholarship has a great contribution to make in the ecumenical process, it must not be allowed to distract us from the essential question, which is, not how deep were the disagreements at the time when Churches separated but to what extent the Holy Spirit has brought them to agreement in faith today. If we have ecumenical hope, we will expect to find essential agreement if we can only uncover it, and be surprised and disappointed if we fail to find it, rather than the reverse.

Another group of ecumenical virtues consists of humility, self-denial, and forbearance. St. Paul's exhortation to the Philippians has an ecumenical application:

> Do nothing from selfishness or conceit, but in humility count others better than yourselves. Let each of you look not only to his own interests, but also to the interests of others (Phil 2:34).

Paul puts before us the model of Jesus himself for whom to be God was a reason not for self-importance and self-seeking but for self-sacrifice:

> Have this mind among yourselves, which is yours in Christ Jesus, who, though he was in the form of God, did not think equality with God a thing to be grasped, but emptied himself, taking the form of a servant (2:57).

Reconciliation of Memories

As applied to ecumenism, this means, as we have already seen, that jealousy of the success of other Churches is unchristian; on the contrary, we should rejoice in their successes. The Anglican cochairman of ARCIC II has written of the need for a "reconciliation of memories"; we must free ourselves from the history of rivalry with which many of us have been brought up. Similarly, in 1979 Pope John Paul II and the Patriarch Dimitrios of Constantinople in a Joint Declaration spoke of the need for the "purification of the collective memory." In the same spirit, the religious correspondent of the London *Times* has suggested that the members of the various Churches should adopt one another's saints and heroes. Moreover, in our dealings with other Churches we must, whenever truth allows, put their interests before our own. Although respect for God's truth does not permit us to abandon what faith tells us is part of God's revelation, we have no right to impose on other Churches, as a condition for reunion, anything which is not an essential to that revelation. As Pope John Paul II has said, we must not fasten unnecessary burdens on other Churches' backs. We must not make it unnecessarily hard for Christians to be reunited.

Attachment to Own Tradition

A further quality that ecumenists need is a firm attachment to their own tradition. Any proposed agreement which requires a Church to abandon or compromise its essential beliefs is likely to be eventually rejected by that Church, with the result that disappointment and resentment are felt on the other side, too. Christians have no right to discard any aspect of the truth that God has entrusted to their own Church. An ecumenist may never be a freethinker; if he or she ceases to think as a faithful member of the Church, that person ceases to be an ecumenist.

Patience

N.B.

The list of ecumenical virtues could be greatly extended. We must content ourselves with mentioning one more, namely, the virtue of patience. Closing the Week of Prayer for Church Unity in 1975, Pope Paul VI spoke of the danger that impatience could lead to the over-simplification of the ecumenical process:

> The heart that loves is always hasty. If our haste is not heeded, love itself makes us suffer. . . . We are aware of the laws of history, which call for a longer period of time than that of our human existence, and it is understandable that the slowness in reaching solutions should seem to make our desires, our attempts, our efforts, and our prayers vain. Let us accept this economy of the divine plan, and let us resolve humbly to persevere.

At the time when I am writing this, it is commonplace to say that there is a general feeling that ecumenism has run out of steam or run into the sand. It is certainly true that the momentum of the first years after Vatican II is not being maintained, but then we have no right to expect that schisms which have become deeply rooted over several centuries can be ended in a few years.

Ecumenism, like so many other human processes, has its phases and rhythms, its times for rapid progress, and its times for slow consolidation, even its times for the endurance of apparent regressions. Relations between Roman Catholics and Anglicans seem to be, as I write this in February 1989, in the third phase. The breakthrough which began with Vatican II, the meeting of the Archbishop of Canterbury and the Pope in 1966, the setting up of ARCIC, and the publication of the ARCIC agreements, were followed by a period of consolidation when the work was publicized and assessed. But now we have reached a stage when in some respects the Churches seem further apart than when they began the process. Not only are there the new problems concerning the ordination of women, first as priests and then as bishops; there has also crystalized the problem of authority insofar as it is unclear if there is any process possible by which the Anglican Communion as a whole and the Roman Catholic Church can commit themselves to an agreement on faith of any sort. This present time seems to call for the dogged virtues of perseverance, patience, and unwearying hope.*

Editor's note*
   Archbishop Runcie and Pope John Paul II met again in Rome and on October 2, 1989 signed a joint declaration affirming efforts for re-union. In the *Episcopalian* for November, 1989, Archbishop Runcie is quoted as having no problem with the pope being a world-wide spiritual leader.

Chapter 3

DIVERSITY AND UNIFORMITY

When the Catholic Church was making preparations for the canonization of the Forty Martyrs of England and Wales, there were fears that other Churches might resent the process on the grounds that it would encourage the continuation of old grudges and rivalries. In order to allay these misgivings, Pope Paul VI at the last minute added the following passage to the address he gave at the canonization ceremony:

> There will be no seeking to lessen the legitimate prestige and the worthy patrimony of piety and usage proper to the Anglican Church when the Roman Catholic Church—this humble "Servant of the servants of God"—is able to embrace her ever-beloved sister in the one authentic communion of the family of Christ: a communion of origin and of faith, a communion of priesthood and of rule, a communion of the saints in the freedom and love of the Spirit of Jesus.

United, Not Absorbed

In a later chapter we shall return to the implications of the term "sister" when applied to another Church. What concerns us here is the promise that there is no question of asking Anglicans to renounce their "worthy patrimony of piety and usage" for the sake of reunion. In other words, a reunited Church need not be a uniform Church. The principle is not new. At the Malines Conversations in the 1920s, Cardinal Mercier and Dom Lambert Beauduin proposed as their aim an Anglican Communion "united but not absorbed."

The Decree on Ecumenism of Vatican II recognized that diversity could have a positive value.

> While preserving unity in essentials, let everyone in the Church, according to the office entrusted to him, preserve a proper freedom in the various forms of spiritual life and discipline, in the variety of liturgical rites, and even in the theological elaborations of revealed truth. In all things let charity prevail. If they are true to this course of action, they will be giving ever richer expression to the authentic catholicity and apostolicity of the Church (n. 4).

The same document made the point even more forcefully with regard to the Orthodox Churches:

> It is of supreme importance to understand, venerate, preserve, and foster the rich liturgical and spiritual heritage of the Eastern Churches in order faithfully to preserve the fullness of Christian tradition (n. 15).

Cardinal Jan Willebrands, the President of the Vatican Secretariat for Christian Unity, entered more deeply into the understanding of Christian diversity in a sermon preached in Cambridge in 1970. In this sermon he indicated the value of the existence within the Church of a number of *typoi* or species of Christian life.

Where there is a long, coherent tradition, commanding one's love and loyalty, creating and sustaining a harmonious and organic whole of complementary elements, each of which supports and strengthens the other, you have the reality of a *typos*.

A "type" in this sense is a combination of "complementary elements" such as a theological method, liturgy, spirituality, canon law. It is the fruit of "a long, coherent tradition" and therefore is not to be lightly modified. Since the elements combine to form "a harmonious and organic whole," the Cardinal is obviously not recommending that the Christian should shop around the Churches in search of an ecumenical cocktail. His point, on the contrary, is that Christ's Church benefits from the existence of a variety of "types."

Need for Diversity

If a typology of Churches—a diversity in unity and unity in diversity—multiplies the possibilities of identifying and celebrating the presence of God in the world, if it brings nearer the hope of providing an imaginative framework within which Christian witness can transform human consciousness for today, then it has all the justification it needs.

It is not difficult to see why such diversity in unity within the Church is not only tolerable but even desirable. The human mind with its limitations is incapable of comprehending the infinite richness of the truth about God and God's dealings with the human race. This would clearly be true if God had left us to our own intellectual devices without the help of revelation. Even after God's definitive self-revelation in the person of Jesus Christ, it remains true that God exceeds human capacity to know God. We therefore need many different attempts to understand God so that a composite picture can be built up.

A single photograph of a building or a face often fails to convey the full quality of the subject; we need a number of photographs taken from different angles before the subject can be grasped in its full splendor. In the 1960s when the work of French Jesuit theologian and scientist Pierre Teilhard de Chardin was becoming popular, a portrait of him was often reproduced, showing him in full face, conveying the impression of thin, poetic features, dominated by a long, sensitive nose. It was only when one saw the much-less-well-known portrait taken in profile that one observed that that poetic nose was a curved, aquiline, patrician beak.

One knows Teilhard better through having seen his face from both angles. So too, God is better known through being reflected in the liturgical splendor of the Orthodox, the warm and simple spontaneity of the Methodist, the dignified restraint of the Anglican, as well as the conceptual clarity and canonical firmness of the Roman Catholic.

It has long been recognized that such diversity is to be found and encouraged within the Roman Catholic Church itself. In liturgy, there is the variety of Latin and Oriental rites and many different styles of putting the former into practice. The variety of spirituality is shown by the large number of religious orders, each with its own charism, which many share with lay associates. In doctrine, there have traditionally been a number of "schools" of theology: Thomist, Scotist, and Augustinian, for example, according to which the truths of revelation are interpreted in a number of different ways. Pope John XXIII, at the beginning of the Second Vatican Council, conveyed this truth in simple terms when he said that

> the substance of the ancient doctrine of the deposit of faith is one thing and the way in which it is presented is another.

What is new is the recognition that a similar diversity could exist between Catholics and other Churches. Recent popes, in their relations with the leaders of other Churches, have often spoken of the need for such interchurch diversity and seen that it applies not only to liturgy, canon law, and spirituality but even to the understanding of doctrine.

Pope Paul VI, for example, preaching in 1972 in the presence of a delegation from the Ecumenical Patriarch of Constantinople, recalled with approval St. Cyprian's conception of the Church as

> a composite and articulated body in which parts and groups can be modeled in particular typical forms, and functions can be distinct though fraternal and converging. Here [in Rome], in the heart of unity and at the center of catholicity, we dream of the living beauty of the Bride of Christ, the Church, wrapped in her many-colored garment (Ps 45:14), clothed, we mean, in a legitimate pluralism of traditional expressions.

Pope Paul, in his reference to "particular typical forms" (*forme tipiche particolari*) and "traditional expressions," seems to be lending his support to Cardinal Willebrands' advocacy, two years earlier, of a diversity of *typoi* in a united Church.

Pope John Paul II has spoken in similar terms concerning the acceptability and the need of pluriformity in the Church. In June

1979, addressing a Coptic delegation on the subject of dialogue between Churches, he spoke as follows:

> Fundamental to this dialogue is the recognition that the richness of this unity in faith and spiritual life has to be expressed in diversity of forms. Unity, whether on the universal level or the local level, does not mean uniformity or absorption of one group by another.

The reference to "faith" indicates that the Pope is envisaging a diversity of doctrinal formulations, as well as of liturgy and spirituality.

Development of Doctrines

Another form of diversity in the Church follows from its existence in history. As Newman saw so clearly, doctrines, like all human ideas, develop. The Vatican Congregation for the Doctrine of the Faith in 1973 drew attention to this principle in its document on the Church entitled *Mysterium Ecclesiae*. The Congregation spoke of the "historical condition" of doctrinal statements and implied that the particular form of words in which a dogma is expressed is not necessarily the best possible expression for all time nor does it preclude other statements of the truth in different terms. The document points out that dogmas are formulated in words whose meaning can change over the years, and are intended to solve questions which may no longer be live issues for later generations.

Moreover, it sometimes happens that some dogmatic truth is first expressed incompletely (but not falsely), and at a later date, when considered in a broader context of faith or human knowledge, it receives a fuller and more perfect expression.

Cardinal Joseph Ratzinger has recently shown that this incompleteness of dogmas has sometimes been due to the separation of Churches. These divisions, he states, have caused the doctrinal decisions of the Catholic Church to suffer from "a certain particularization both as to language and thought." In other words, the Catholic perception of the truth has been handicapped through being deprived of the insights of other Churches. The interpretation of dogmas, therefore, demands the practice of ecumenical dialogue:

> Unity is a fundamental hermeneutic principle of all theology, and we must learn to read the documents which have been handed down to us according to the hermeneutics of unity, which show up much that is new and open doors where only bolts were visible before. . . . To opt out and cut oneself off [from ecumenical dialogue] means artificial withdrawal into a past beyond recall; it means restricting tradition to the past.

The two popes quoted above applied this understanding of doctrinal diversity to resolving the traditional differences between Catholics and the non-Chalcedonian Churches. These Churches, for complex historical reasons, have never subscribed to the Christological definition of the Council of Chalcedon of 451 which taught that the one Person of the incarnate Son of God, Jesus Christ, existed in two natures, that of God and that of man. Because they rejected the two-nature formula, these non-Chalcedonian Churches—which include the Copts, the Armenians, and the Syrian Orthodox—are sometimes called Monophysites or believers in one nature. Thus in 1971, Pope Paul VI published a Common Declaration with the Patriarch of the Syrian Orthodox Church in which the two leaders stated their agreement that

> there is no difference in the faith they profess concerning the mystery of the Word of God made flesh and become really man, even if over the centuries difficulties have risen out of the different theological expressions by which this faith was expressed.

Eight years later, Pope John Paul II was to apply the same principle to the Egyptian Coptic Church, on the occasion that has been referred to above. Like his predecessor, he affirmed that, while each Church remained faithful to its traditional formulations of the doctrine of Christ, God

> permits us to profess today our common faith in Jesus Christ, his divine Son, true God and true man. . . . We rejoice together that the doubts and suspicions of the past have been overcome so that

with full hearts we can proclaim together once again this fundamental truth of our Christian faith.

So far, we have been considering the need for diversity in the Church, even diversity of statements of doctrine, if our understanding of revelation is not to be unnecessarily limited. But, as the argument has unfolded, it has become evident that the principle applies to the search for Christian unity. Two conclusions can be drawn.

Search for Agreement

First, the dialogue of Churches seeking unity should not be aimed at inducing one Church or the other to abandon its traditional doctrines in favor of those of the other Church. The correct procedure is illustrated by the statements we have considered which emerged from the dialogue between Catholics and non-Chalcedonians. After each party has listened sympathetically while the other explains its beliefs, together they should try to discover to what extent different theological formulations conceal underlying agreement. If the result is positive, each Church can continue to follow its traditions in the confidence that the other acknowledges their truth. This is what happened in the fourth century when St. Hilary and St. Athanasius each discovered, apparently independently, that the two ways of describing the relationship of God the Son to God the Father, by calling him either "of the same being" (*homoousios*) or "of similar being" (*homoiousios*), should not be seen as mutually exclusive since either form of words, if properly understood, could be used in an orthodox sense.

The second conclusion is that the doctrinal unity to be sought is what the Anglican-Roman Catholic International Commission called "substantial agreement." By this, the Commission meant unanimous agreement of all its members "on essential matters where it considers that doctrine admits no divergence." In an earlier explanation of the meaning of substantial agreement, ARCIC stated its expectation that "if there are any remaining points of disagreement they can be resolved on the principles here established."

Such remaining points may be of two kinds. On the one hand, the points of disagreement may be such that eventual agreement is to be hoped for on the basis of what has already been agreed upon. For example, on the basis of the agreement reached by ARCIC II concerning justification by faith, it is to be hoped that agreement can in time be reached concerning the Roman Catholic doctrine of indulgences, concerning which agreement has not yet been reached.

On the other hand, the points of disagreement may be such that agreement over them is not necessary. In other words, there may be "a variety of theological approaches" in a united Church. This is the basis of the agreements reached between Catholics and non-Chalcedonians: in order to agree on the basic truth about Jesus Christ that he is true God and true man, it is not necessary to reach agreement over the question whether this duality is best expressed in terms of two natures.

ARCIC I believed that another example of agreement on essentials coexisting with disagreement over "theological approaches" was to be found in the diversity of views concerning devotion paid to the reserved Blessed Sacrament. After first indicating a line of agreement on the grounds that

> adoration of Christ in the reserved sacrament should be regarded as an extension of Eucharistic worship, even though it does not include immediate sacramental reception, which remains the primary purpose of reservation,

the Commission had to record that some Anglicans still found any adoration paid to Christ in the reserved sacrament "unacceptable" on the grounds that it suggested "too static and localized a presence" of Christ. Nevertheless, the Commission felt justified in affirming

> that there can be a divergence in matters of practice and in theological judgments relating to them, without destroying a common Eucharistic faith, illustrates what we mean by substantial agreement. Differences of theology and practice may well coexist with

a real consensus on the essentials of Eucharistic faith as in fact they do within each of our communions.

Hierarchy of Truths

What has been said here about diversity in the formulation of doctrines comes close to the statement in the Vatican II Decree on Ecumenism on the "hierarchy of truths":

> Furthermore, in ecumenical dialogue, Catholic theologians, standing fast by the teaching of the Church yet searching together with separated brethren into the divine mysteries, should do so with love for the truth, with charity, and with humility. When comparing doctrines with one another, they should remember that in Catholic doctrine there exists an order or "hierarchy" of truths, since they vary in their relation to the foundation of the Christian faith. Thus the way will be opened whereby this kind of "fraternal rivalry" will incite all to a deeper realization and a clearer expression of the unfathomable riches of Christ (n. 11).

This statement is of such importance that care must be taken to interpret it correctly. The Council implies a distinction between fundamental doctrines, about which there must be agreement if there is to be genuine reunion between Churches, and doctrines which are not fundamental in this sense, about which difference of understanding can exist without undermining basic unity in faith. It might therefore be argued that doctrines of this second kind are not matters of faith at all but only matters of opinion. It is unlikely that this is what the Council meant. Even nonfundamental doctrines are said to bear a "relation to the foundation of the Christian faith," and therefore seem to be envisaged as expressions of faith themselves.

It is more plausible to interpret the passage in the following way. Doctrines which are held as of faith can differ in degree (in an "order" or "hierarchy"). Some are formulated explicitly in terms of the foundation of faith, namely, about Jesus Christ and the salvation which the threefold God brings about through him. Other articles of faith, such as those concerned with the Blessed Virgin Mary, may not be formulated explicitly in such terms.

Nevertheless, as all faith is ultimately faith in Jesus Christ, such non-Christological doctrines must be indirectly expressions of faith in him even though they are formulated in other terms and may be connected with the truths about Jesus Christ only by implication.

This affirmation of the hierarchy of truths by the Council has an ecumenical relevance. Before Churches come to doctrinal agreement, it will cause no surprise if beliefs with a lower place in the hierarchy of truths are seen by one Church to be articles of faith, which express the fundamental truths of God, Christ, and salvation, though only indirectly, and by the other to be only theological opinions (sometimes called *theologoumena*). But is it justifiable for two Churches, while taking these different views about a doctrine which comes low in the hierarchy of truths, to claim nevertheless to share the same faith? This is a question to which we shall return in Chapter 6 in relation to Catholic doctrine concerning the Blessed Virgin Mary.

Limits of Diversity

So far in this chapter our discussion has concentrated on the possibility and even the desirability of a variety of doctrinal traditions within a united Church. We have now been brought to the point where we must shift our viewpoint and consider the limits of diversity. When does an appeal to the hierarchy of truths cease to be justified? How can one distinguish between legitimate diversity and a fragmented indifferentism? There are several cohesive factors which prevent the Church from disintegrating into a shapeless multiformity.

First, the Church must constantly refer back to the source and the criterion of its faith, namely Jesus Christ, as mediated through the Scriptures and the Church's teaching. Secondly, these foundations of the Church's faith are not dead history but a living tradition which we hold not as so many individuals, but as members of a community. In the words of ARCIC I,

> Shared commitment and belief create a common mind in determining how the Gospel should be interpreted and obeyed.

This is the reason why in English-speaking countries the recitation of the Creed at Mass begins with the words, not "I believe," but "We believe." Thirdly, the faith of the community within which one believes and by which one measures one's own faith is not primarily the ability to understand certain verbal statements of a doctrine and to recognize their truth but rather a shared relationship with Christ, especially in prayer, both private and liturgical. This is one application of the traditional principle that there is a connection between the way we pray and the way we believe: *lex orandi, lex credendi.* Fourthly, the community has been equipped with the teaching authority of the ordained ministry to articulate its faith and so to be the means by which the Holy Spirit leads the Church into all the truth (cf. John 16:13). Fifthly, for a Roman Catholic the shared faith is the faith of a worldwide body of those in communion with the Bishop of Rome. The strength of the ties of communion with Rome provides a firm framework within which a lively pluralism can flourish.

Chapter 4

DEGREES OF COMMUNION

We saw in the first chapter that unity is an inalienable property of Christ's Church. Despite their evident divisions, Christians are already united. We saw too that, as Vatican II envisaged the Church, this unity is focused in a special way in the Roman Catholic Church through which "we believe that our Lord entrusted all the blessings of the New Covenant." The statement of the Council's Constitution on the Church, that Christ's Church "subsists in" the Roman Catholic Church (n. 8), is developed in the Decree on Ecumenism in terms of unity:

> The unity of the one and only Church, which Christ bestowed on his Church from the beginning . . . subsists in the [Roman] Catholic Church as something she can never lose (n. 4).

What Constitutes a Church?

Nevertheless, this already-existing unity focused on the Roman Catholic Church embraces also the other Christian Churches. In the words of the Vatican II Decree on Ecumenism,

> Those who believe in Christ and have been properly baptized are put in some, though imperfect, communion with the Catholic Church (n. 3).

45

What form does this imperfect communion take? The Anglican members of ARCIC I put this question in different terms, asking if,

> as long as a Church is not in communion with the Bishop of Rome it is regarded by the Roman Catholic Church as less than fully a Church.

This is a difficult question to answer, not least because there is no obvious criterion for deciding what "being a Church" means. An answer cannot be readily found in the New Testament. The writers there apply the term "Church" to local communities. St. Paul, for example, writes of "the Church of the Laodiceans" (Col 4:16). They also speak of the universal "Church"; it is in this sense that Jesus promised to build his Church on Peter (Matt 16:18) and that St. Paul spoke of Christ as "the head of the body, the Church" (Col 1:8). But the New Testament never uses the term "Church" in the sense in which we speak of the Anglican Church, the Methodist Church, or even the Church of England, i.e., at the intermediate level of a group of local communities united by common traditions and a common structure of authority. To use the word "Church" in this sense has no scriptural precedent. This does not mean that we should abandon such a convenient expression, simply that it is not clear from the New Testament what we should mean by it.

The Decree on Ecumenism used the word "Churches" to denote the Eastern Orthodox but when speaking of the separated bodies of the West spoke more cautiously of "Churches and ecclesial communities" (nn. 15, 19). It did not state explicitly what it understood the difference between Churches and ecclesial communities to be, but it did drop some hints. Of the Orthodox Churches, it is said that they "possess true sacraments . . . by apostolic succession," above all the priesthood and the Eucharist. Consequently, Roman Catholics are encouraged to worship in common with them in suitable circumstances (n. 15). Of the separated bodies of the West, however, it is said that "they have not preserved the proper reality of the Eucharistic mystery in its fullness, especially because of the absence of the sacrament of

Orders" (n. 22). Presumably this is reason why Roman Catholics are given no explicit encouragement to join them in worship (though the 1967 *Ecumenical Directory* is much more forthcoming). However, the use of the phrase "Churches and ecclesial communities" shows that one cannot simply conclude that none of the Western bodies is regarded as a Church.

Accordingly, it seems possible for a Roman Catholic to speak of a body as a Church at the intermediate level with which we are concerned, in three senses. First, the expression could be nothing more than a courteous way of speaking of it in the terms that body chooses for itself, without answering the question whether it is in fact part of the true Church of Christ. Secondly, in calling a community a Church, one might imply that, as a body, it contains "the elements of sanctification and truth" which belong to Christ's Church, such as the Scriptures, baptism, priesthood, and the Eucharist. Thirdly, one might mean that, together with the Roman Catholic Church, it is a part of the visible reality in which the Church of Christ "subsists" in the Roman Catholic Church. Clearly, the Roman Catholic Church sees other bodies as more than Churches in the first, polite sense; on the other hand, for reasons explained in Chapter 1, it is not yet possible to recognize them as Churches in the third sense as long as they are not yet in full communion with the Bishop of Rome. What needs further investigation is the extent to which they can be called Churches in the second sense, insofar as they are, as bodies, endowed with the elements of sanctification and truth. In other words, just as there are degrees of communion, so too there are degrees of "Churchness."

Scripture as a Basis for Communion

The passage in the Decree on Ecumenism on imperfect communion quoted at the beginning of this chapter, indicates two bases for this communion: belief in Christ and true baptism. We shall consider these bases shortly. But first, attention should be given to another basis, namely, possession of the same Scripture, for Scripture is the source of our knowledge of Christ and the guarantee of our practice of baptism.

ARCIC I, in its treatment of *koinonia* (communion), states that

> the *koinonia* is grounded in the word of God preached, believed, and obeyed.

Nevertheless, from the first centuries Christians have discovered that the same Scriptures can lead to widely different interpretations. Consequently, if communion based on possession of the same Scriptures is to be more than an abstraction, there must be some procedure for reaching a common understanding of their application to urgent contemporary problems. As early as the Council of Jerusalem described in the Acts of the Apostles (chapter 15), where the first Christians decided not to impose the observances of Judaism on pagan converts, we see assemblies making binding decisions about the implications of the Bible. From the second century, there is evidence of local councils acting in this way; the first universal council, that of Nicaea, to do the same was held in the fourth century.

However, the Churches do not agree about the procedures to be adopted for reaching internal agreement concerning the interpretation of Scripture and its application to new situations. Thus, for Roman Catholics the Pope performs a similar function in defining the Church's mind to that played by the Councils of the early Church. Anglicans on the other hand rely more on authority which is dispersed throughout the whole Church rather than that which is concentrated on officeholders. Nevertheless, even though the Churches have adopted different organs of authority, and even though in some important matters they differ in their actual interpretations of Scripture, the very fact that Scripture is accepted as a revealed source and test of belief, and as God's Word which is to be understood and obeyed and proclaimed in public worship, is a strong foundation of communion among them.

Two Other Bases of Communion

The first of the bases of communion mentioned by the Decree on Ecumenism was a shared belief in Jesus Christ. All Christians venerate Jesus Christ and have faith in him as the Savior and to that extent are in communion. However, this community of faith, like the acceptance of common Scriptures, can exist in different degrees. Not all who call themselves Christians nowadays are prepared to confess Jesus as truly God as well as truly man, as the Council of Chalcedon taught. Certainly, many different views exist among Christians concerning the precise understanding of the way in which we owe to Christ our salvation, and concerning the sense in which it is to be believed that he rose from the dead. Nevertheless, all who at least regard Christ as God's unique and conclusive mediator of salvation are united in a basic faith.

The other basis of communion which the Decree lists is the sharing of a common baptism.

All who have been justified by faith in baptism are incorporated into Christ; they therefore have a right to be called Christians and with good reason are accepted as brothers and sisters by the children of the Catholic Church (n. 3):

> Baptism . . . constitutes the sacramental bond of unity existing among all who through it are reborn (n. 22).

Though stating that there may be "reasonable doubt about the baptism conferred [by other Christians] in some particular case"—there are instances, for example, of baptism conferred without water or without the use of the name of the Father, Son, and Holy Spirit—the Catholic Church recognizes the validity of the baptisms of all the major Christian Churches and forbids rebaptism.

Faith and Order, the ecumenical theological body linked with the World Council of Churches, in 1982 published a joint statement on baptism as part of the Lima Report entitled "Baptism, Eucharist, and Ministry." Representatives of all the main denominations, including the Roman Catholic Church, participated. Nevertheless, the document showed that, despite wide agreement as to the theology of baptism and its practice, the extent to which baptism is a basis of communion also admits of degrees.

Differences Regarding Baptism

The most obvious difference concerns the practice of baptizing babies. Some Churches, of which the Baptists constitute the best-known example, maintain that baptism should only be received with faith and free consent. Among those who practice "believer's baptism" in this way, some would also insist that infant baptism is no true baptism, so that those who have been baptized as babies need to be baptized again as believers; though, to speak accurately, this would not involve baptizing again as in this view the infant "baptism" is not a baptism at all. Others from these Churches would accept the recommendation of the Lima document that, while maintaining their own practice of believer's baptism, they should accept baptism received in infancy as a true, unrepeatable baptism but should require, as all Churches should, that those baptized as babies should be given a Christian upbringing which prepares them to conceive a free faith in Christ when they grow up. Such a mature act of faith would be a free endorsement of the decision which the Christian congregation made to accept responsibility for them in admitting them as babies into the community of believers.

There is, however, a deeper problem concerning the acceptance of baptism as one of the bases of communion. In accepting the baptism of another Church, one is not merely saying that those baptized in that Church receive as individuals the graces which the sacrament confers. Baptism is not merely a means of grace but a sacrament of initiation by which one becomes a member of the Church in question and thereby becomes a part of Christ's Body, which is the Church. Consequently, to recognize another Church's baptism is to recognize that that Church is part of Christ's Church. Thus far, we are simply considering from another viewpoint the question raised by the Roman Catholic Church concerning the status of Christian bodies not in communion with itself. A new problem, however, arises in connection with baptism. Can one recognize the validity of the baptism conferred in another body, and therefore that body's reality as a church, without recognizing its other sacraments of confirmation and Eucharist? For baptism is not the only sacrament by which one becomes a member of the Church; recent Roman Catholic documents affirm that there are two other sacraments of initiation, i.e., confirmation and first communion. The problem extends further; though baptism by a lay person is generally considered to be valid, one cannot recognize the confirmation and Eucharist of another Church without *ipso facto* recognizing that Church's ordained ministry. The argument can be summarized thus: if baptism, then Church; if Church, then confirmation and Eucharist; if confirmation and Eucharist, then valid orders.

The problem can be formulated in another way. To acknowledge a Church's baptism is to recognize that its members, *as members of that Church*, belong to the Body of Christ. But all baptized members of Christ's Body, provided they have not cut themselves off from the Body by serious sin, have the right and the need to receive the Body of Christ in the Eucharist. It follows then that recognition of baptism involves recognition of Eucharist and therefore of ordained ministry.

Three Possible Solutions

It seems clear, then, that the spirit of ecumenism has moved Churches to recognize one another's baptism without fully exploring the implications of that recognition. If this is so, three different conclusions might be drawn. The first would be that, if one is unable to extend that recognition to Eucharist and orders, recognition of baptism should be withdrawn until the theological implications have been more fully examined. The second would be that the inconsistency should be removed by the recognition of the orders and Eucharist of all Churches whose baptism one acknowledges. If it is judged, as I personally would judge, that the first solution must be rejected because it involves the reversal of years of ecumenical progress which the consensus of nearly all Churches sees as the work of the Holy Spirit and that the second solution must be rejected on the grounds that it overlooks the reasons which have led some Churches to be cautious about recognizing the orders and the Eucharist of some other Churches, then one must seek a third solution.

This third solution would involve acknowledging that the recognition of another Church's baptism, like the recognition of its possession of the Scriptures and of its faith in Jesus Christ, admits of degrees. What the Decree on Ecumenism has in mind is the possibility of a limited recognition of baptism, such that it is held to be a true sacrament which must not be repeated for people who enter into full communion with the Roman Catholic Church, even though this recognition does not necessarily carry with it the recognition of the Eucharist and the ordination of the Church in question, and therefore leaves open the problem of how fully the Church in question participates in the means of salvation with which Christ endowed his Church.

The Decree on Ecumenism favors this third solution. Although baptism unites Christians across Church divisions,

> baptism, of itself, is only a beginning, a point of departure. Baptism is thus ordained toward a complete profession of faith, a complete incorporation into the system of salvation such as Christ himself willed it to be, and finally, toward a complete integration into Eucharistic communion. . . . The ecclesial communities separated from us lack the fullness of unity with us which flows from baptism (n. 22).

This raises further the question why the Roman Catholic Church is unable simply to recognize the ordinations and, by implication, the Eucharist, of all other Churches whose baptism it recognizes. In answer to this question, it will first be helpful to remove possible misconceptions. The reason why Roman Catholics do not recognize the orders of many other Churches is not the simple one that there can be no valid ordinations outside the Roman Catholic Church, for Rome has always recognized the orders of the Orthodox. Nor is the nonrecognition a judgment which could be changed as a gesture of good will. Recognition of orders cannot be brought about by an arbitrary decision. It requires either the acknowledgment that, as a matter of objective fact, valid orders already exist in the Church in question or else the performance of some sacramental act which will make those orders valid.

Obstacles to Mutual Recognition of Ministries

The considerations which have always prevented Rome from acknowledging the existence of true ordination in most Protestant Churches are easy to understand. If orders have to be transmitted in apostolic succession from the apostles and if the only valid channel of the apostolic succession is the line of bishop, it follows at once that the orders in Churches which do not have bishops cannot be acknowledged to be valid. Much more complicated are the reasons which have led the Roman Catholic Church to pass a similar judgment on Anglican orders even though that Church is an episcopal one. It has made this judgment consistently since the time of the Reformation and reaffirmed it with great emphasis in 1896, when Pope Leo XIII, being asked to give a formal decision, stated in the Apostolic Letter *Apostolicae Curae* the conclusion that ''ordinations performed according to the Anglican rite have been and are completely null and totally void (*irritas prorsus . . . omninoque nullas*).''

The Pope put forward three reasons for his unfavorable verdict—first, the argument from precedent: from the beginning Rome had treated Anglican orders as invalid and in 1896 there seemed no sufficient reason for Rome to change its mind; secondly, the argument from lack of due intention: the bishops who performed the first episcopal ordinations in the reign of Elizabeth I did not have the intention required for administering the sacrament validly because they expressly intended not to ordain priests who would offer the sacrifice of the Mass; thirdly, the argument from defective form: a form of words which omitted all reference to Eucharistic sacrifice was deliberately adopted at the beginning of the same reign. For all these reasons, the Pope concluded, the line of apostolic succession was broken in the sixteenth century, and subsequent changes in the rite cannot repair it.

Solutions to Problem of Apostolic Succession

This problem constitutes a major obstacle which limits the extent to which the Roman Catholic and Anglican Churches can make progress toward unity. When Pope John Paul II and the Archbishop of Canterbury, Dr. Robert Runcie, set up the second Anglican-Roman Catholic International Commission in 1982, they placed this issue on the commission's agenda. Commentators have proposed several possible ways of finding a solution. The first would be for Rome to institute a new inquiry which would reappraise the process of 1896. This might be done on two grounds. On the one hand, one might attempt to show that there were flaws in the arguments put forward in 1896; on the other, one might maintain that a degree of bias or irregularity in the conduct of the inquiry invalidates the verdict. Such a new inquiry, however, would inescapably carry the risk that Rome might after all see no good reason for changing its mind or at best might come up with a verdict of "not proven" instead of an outright condemnation. In either case, the result would be much disappointment and bitterness.

A second solution would be to try to show that circumstances had changed so much since 1896 that, whether the verdict of *Apostolicae Curae* was correct or not, it no longer applied nearly one hundred years later. ARCIC I stated its belief that its agreed statements on Eucharist and Ministry, if accepted by the two Churches, constituted a "new context" for the reevaluation of Pope Leo's verdict. Cardinal Willebrands has suggested a way in which this new context might be established. In a letter to the cochairmen of ARCIC II, he recommended that the ordination rites currently in use in the Anglican Communion throughout the world should be examined to see if they represent ARCIC's understanding of Eucharist and Ministry. If the results are positive, and if both Churches endorse ARCIC's theology, Leo XIII's arguments from defect of intention and form will have been shown no longer to have relevance to the contemporary situation. There would still remain, however, the alleged breach in the apostolic succession. For that reason, work on the lines suggested by Cardinal Willebrands will need to be linked with work on the third or fourth solutions.

The third solution would concentrate on the problem of the apostolic succession. Many Anglican bishops have had among their consecrators a bishop from a Church whose orders Rome recognizes, such as the Old Catholic Church or the Polish National Church in the United States. In fact, it has been argued that all the bishops of the Church of England at least have in this way been ordained in the apostolic succession. However, I have heard it said with great emphasis by dedicated Anglican ecumenists that no solution can be found along these lines. It would not be honest, they believe, for reunion between Rome and Canterbury to be based on apostolic succession maintained in another, much smaller body.

Accordingly, it seems that a fourth method of healing the alleged breach in the apostolic succession will have to be sought. This would consist of a rite which was intended as the conferring of an ordination if, and only if, in the eyes of God, such an ordination were necessary. In practice, this would be a conditional ordination of the Anglican bishops and other clergy. Although the first Lambeth Conference to be held after the First World War with great generosity professed its willingness to accept such a solution, many Anglicans today are unable in conscience to accept it, as experience has convinced them of the validity of their ministry. Consequently, it may be necessary to search for some rite which will satisfy the Roman request for a sacramental ordination which will heal the breach in the succession, while not involving loss of integrity on the Anglican side. The procedure adopted at the establishment of the Church of North India in 1970 might offer a way forward. When this Church was founded from the union of an Episcopal Church (the Anglican) with a number of Churches without bishops, there was a mutual laying on of hands which was intended to supply anything that in the eyes of God needed supplying to the orders of the Churches involved. As far as the Anglicans were concerned, the rite performed by Anglican bishops reestablished apostolic succession in the other Churches. The same procedure might be adopted to meet Roman Catholic misgivings about a lack of apostolicity in Anglican orders. If there were Anglican objections to the apparent one-sidedness of this solution, Roman Catholics should recognize that they too had a lack to be supplied, namely, a defect of catholicity. The mutual laying on of hands would be a sign not of conditional ordination conferred on the Roman Catholic clergy but of the restoration of their ministry to communion with the Anglican Church. Moreover, it would be worth considering whether the rite could be made more acceptable by being performed only for selected leaders with the understanding that this would be a representative or collegial act with sacramental consequences for all the clergy of each Church.

Ordination of Women

There remains, however, a further obstacle in the way of the mutual recognition of ministries, namely, the ordination of women to the presbyterate in several provinces of the Anglican Communion and now to the episcopate in the United States. We shall return to this problem in Chapter 6. The question which must be asked for the present is rather this: Can Roman Catholics devise a way of recognizing or validating Anglican orders without changing their own view that women not only may not but cannot be ordained as presbyters, let alone bishops?

If this is not possible, and if neither the Roman Catholic Church nor the Anglican provinces are likely to change their minds, it seems that the two Churches will be stuck with a far-from-complete degree of communion which stops short of a mutual recognition of ordinations, and therefore cannot include intercommunion.

In the *Instruction* which introduces the new Roman Missal, the Eucharist is described as

> the center of the whole Christian life for the universal Church, the local Church, and for each and every one of the faithful.

But it does not follow that if the fullness of communion symbolized by Eucharistic sharing is not an immediate possibility, no progress is possible. ARCIC I spoke of achieving "unity by stages." We must consider these stages in the next chapter.

Chapter 5

REUNION BY STAGES

"I do not ask to see the distant scene," wrote Newman in his poem *Lead, Kindly Light*, "one step enough for me." Christians have no clear idea what form of unity Christ wills for his followers, nor may they see how this goal can be reached. We may not be able to see what the next step but one should be, let alone the distant scene; nevertheless, whatever the problems, there is always some next step which we can take on this journey into the unknown.

Two Plans for a United Church

It might be thought that although the path to unity may be shrouded in fog, we know very well where we are trying to get to. This is not true, however. There are at least two radically different views of the form the united Church might take. The first conception is that of a Church so united that in any place there is one bishop as the focus of its unity while the unity of the worldwide Church is structured by the unity of the college of bishops in communion with the Pope. For example, in Liverpool one of the bishoprics would cease to exist, so that both Anglicans and Roman Catholics would give up their separate identities and become simply fellow members of a united Church in that city under one bishop. In this pattern the unity of the Church would be most evident. The second plan for a united Church, by contrast, is prepared to sacrifice some of the clarity of the first model in order to preserve the different traditions (called "types" in Chapter 2). Thus, both the Roman Catholic and Anglican Churches would continue in their distinctness, each with its own bishop, as reconciled sister Churches in full communion with one another and sharing not only the same Scriptures and faith but being parts of the same organization at the center of which would be the Bishop of Rome as Universal Primate. The second pattern would imply for Anglicans a status such as is already possessed in the Roman Catholic Church by such Churches as the Maronite Church in Lebanon which maintain their distinctive traditions of liturgy, spirituality, and canon law.

The future of the united Church is so remote that it is perhaps idle to speculate which of these two forms it should take. It is surely true, however, that there must be many people in many Churches who, while desiring the unity of Christ's followers, would feel that there are some features in their own Church which they could not in conscience forgo. An Orthodox, for example, is unlikely to move beyond the idea of the Roman and Orthodox Churches continuing to exist as reconciled "sister Churches." An English Roman Catholic is similarly unlikely to entertain the prospect of appearing to become an Anglican. Therefore, at very least it seems that if the first pattern, of one bishop in one place, is to be adopted, this could only be after a period in which the second pattern was accepted as an intermediate stage during which the members of the two Churches could learn to know and trust one another.

In this chapter I shall consider one of the many journeys towards unity, namely, that between Anglicans and Roman Catholics. This is the one that I am most familiar with, having been a member of ARCIC for nearly twenty years. It is a journey still far from completed but one in which much ground has already been covered. There have been periods of rapid progress and other periods of uphill slog, periods when we seemed to see clearly where we were going, and at least one period when all was dark and there seemed no way ahead.

Anglican-Roman Catholic Steps Towards Unity

We can identify as the first step the Vatican II Decree on Ecumenism and the meeting of Pope Paul VI and Archbishop Michael Ramsey in 1966, when they pledged the two Churches to the search for reunion and determined to establish a Commission (eventually called the Anglican-Roman Catholic International Commission) to help to achieve that end. After their meeting, the two leaders issued a Common Declaration setting out their intention to establish formal dialogue between the two Churches. The aim was to promote the full development of "respect, esteem, and fraternal love" between them in the hope of attaining "that unity in truth for which Christ prayed" and "a restoration of complete communion of faith and sacramental life." When ARCIC eventually came into existence to carry this dialogue on, it customarily described the goal which its founding fathers set themselves as that of "full organic unity." The 1966 Declaration recognized that this search for the restoration of full communion was motivated not by considerations of administrative convenience but by Christ's prayer in John 17 for the unity of his followers.

Common Declaration

The Common Declaration also sketched the method which the Commission was later to find so fruitful. There was to be "a serious dialogue . . . founded on the Gospels and on the ancient common traditions." In other words, the discussions were to start with what the two Churches held in common and to follow where that led rather than begin with the investigation of old controversies. One can also find in the statement a general indication of the subjects to be discussed: "not only theological matters such as Scripture, tradition, and liturgy but also matters of practical difficulty felt on either side."

Joint Preparatory Commission

The agenda were worked out in greater detail by a Joint Preparatory Commission which was formed with remarkable rapidity, met three times in 1967 in Italy, England, and Malta and early in 1968 submitted a Report known as the Malta Report. It recommended the setting up of a permanent Commission (the eventual ARCIC) which would have very wide responsibility for relations between the two Churches. In addition, the Report proposed a number of measures which would constitute a second stage in the relationship between the Roman Catholic and Anglican Churches. This new stage would consist of two steps, one theological and the other consisting of a number of practical measures.

Joint Proclamation of Faith

The theological step recommended by the Preparatory Commission would consist in a joint proclamation of faith made by the two Churches. From what has been said in Chapter 3, it will be clear that there is here no suggestion that either of the Churches is called upon to sacrifice its treasured traditional expressions of faith. Nor, the Preparatory Commission states, will either Church be "tied to a positive acceptance of all the beliefs and devotional practices of the other." What is envisaged is a joint affirmation of the

> basic truths set forth in the ecumenical Creeds and the common tradition of the ancient Church.

Anglicans and Roman Catholics alike already accept the authority of the councils of the early Church, hold the Apostles' Creed and the Nicene Creed to be authoritative expressions of faith and incorporate them into the liturgy. For the two Churches to make a formal joint profession of these Creeds would be a public and formal acknowledgment that they hold that

> the Church is founded upon the revelation of God the Father, made known to us in the Person and work of Jesus Christ, who is present through the Holy Spirit in the Scriptures and his Church, and is the only Mediator between God and Man, the ultimate Authority for all our doctrine.

The Commission might have added baptism and the resurrection of the dead to this list of fundamental beliefs included in the Creeds.

It does not, however, follow that only what is contained in these Creeds is a "basic truth." They make no explicit mention of the Eucharist, of ordained ministry, or of the exercise of authority in the Church. It is precisely in these areas that disagreements have existed. Hence, though the Preparatory Commission envisaged the common profession of faith as an immediate step which the two Churches could take, it would not represent complete agreement on every aspect of basic Christian truth. ARCIC has spent many years discussing the problem areas, but the Churches are not yet in a position to say that they hold all their basic beliefs in common. Consequently, an affirmation of agreement on Eucharist, ministry, and authority, and perhaps other doctrines, too, will be possible only at a later stage of the Churches' journey of convergence.

Practical Joint Measures

More than twenty years after the Malta Report, the Churches have still not been able to take this theological step which the Preparatory Commission proposed. In fact, the Report itself has never been officially endorsed. However, the practical measures which the Commission recommended have fared rather better, some of them at any rate having become common practice. First, the Report urged that there should be annual joint meetings of all the bishops of the two Churches in a particular country or region, or at least of a representative number of them. In a small country like Wales, it has proved possible for the two sets of bishops to meet regularly, and the meetings have helped to establish trust and friendship between the two hierarchies. In England, however, there are no regular meetings even of representative groups of bishops. The Malta Report also urged that the leaders of the two Churches should make joint or parallel statements on urgent issues relating to human rights and international relations. Apart from the value which such pronouncements would have as evidence of the close relationship between the two Churches, the secular authorities would find a united Christian voice harder to resist than a divided one.

The Report urged that cooperation between the Churches should extend to other fields. There are many moral and pastoral issues over which the Churches could speak and act more effectively in concert than individually. Even though they are not yet in complete agreement over some moral teachings, for example on the subjects of abortion and contraception, there is probably a greater degree of agreement between them than has been formalized so that some joint action would be both possible and desirable.

Another area in which the Malta Report recommended concerted action by the two Churches is evangelization; that is to say, the attempt to bring the Gospel to unbelievers. The day is long past when the Western Churches could think of evangelization as an activity exclusively to be pursued on "foreign missions," although the Commission does recommend consultation and cooperation in the foreign mission field, which would be a welcome change from the rivalries which have flourished in many regions. But Britain, like many other Western countries, has itself become a mission field, not only in the sense that the number of immigrants has vastly increased but, more significantly, because it is no longer true that Britain is, except in externals, a Christian country. In many ways, the culture we live in is secular or even pagan. Christian practice or even Christian faith belongs only to a minority. Consequently, one of the main tasks, if not *the* main task, of the Christian Churches is to proclaim the Good News of Christ to people in Britain who have not yet come to accept it. The Churches cannot be content simply to nourish the faith of those who already believe. What the Malta Report is recommending is that the proposed new stage of relationship between the two Churches should include cooperation in the evangelistic task. The Churches should be partners in mission. Such partnership involves much more than the renunciation of rivalry. It requires each Church to regard the other's gain as its own, which is possible only if the Churches can accept one another as a true part of the Body of Christ.

Possible Effect on Mixed Marriages

Nowadays in Britain, it is only a relatively small minority of Roman Catholics who marry a partner from their own Church. Consequently, a measure which would affect the lives of many, and which would vividly indicate that a new relationship between the Churches was being inaugurated, would be a change in the arrangements affecting mixed marriages. Since the teaching of the two Churches concerning the theology and ethics of marriage differs in a number of ways, the Preparatory Commission indicated the need for joint study of "the doctrine of marriage in its sacramental dimension, its ethical demands, its canonical status, and its pastoral implications." The Commission also pointed to the need for "acceptable changes in Church regulations" to "alleviate some of the difficulties caused by mixed marriages." Although it did not suggest what these changes might be, experience in the last twenty years has shown that the partners in mixed marriages often suffer great pain from their inability, by Roman Catholic Canon Law, to receive communion regularly together; moreover, further pain is caused by the promise which has to be made by the Catholic partner to do his or her best to bring the children up in the Roman Catholic Church. A change in Roman Catholic law in these two areas could not be made lightly. It would presuppose a large measure of mutual trust and acceptance on the part of the two Churches. For to be content that one's children should be brought up in another Church implies a high estimate of the spiritual value of that Church; moreover, for Roman Catholics at least, shared communion is possible only on the basis of shared faith. Consequently, such a change in regulations would belong to a later stage in the convergence of the two Churches rather than to the first step under discussion.

Possible Effects on Worship

The Preparatory Commission believed that the new stage it was proposing should affect the Churches' worship. They recom-

mended prayer in common and in particular "non-Eucharistic ser-
vices, the exploration of new forms of worship, and retreats in
common." Relationships between religious orders of the two
Churches are encouraged, as is cooperation in liturgical revision.
All of these measures were immediately permissible in 1968 and
could therefore form part of the first step.

Another proposal which would have required a change in
Roman Catholic law, and therefore would fit in better at a later
stage, urged that the *Ecumenical Directory* should be modified so
as to permit "the exchange of preachers for the homily during
the celebration of the Eucharist." In fact, the *Directory* does not
even allow non-Catholics to perform the reading of Scripture at
a Catholic Eucharist or a Catholic to do the same at a non-Catholic
Eucharist. In practice, however, many exceptions seem to be
tolerated.

Shared Theological Training and Research

A last area in which the Commission believed immediate advance could be made is that of theological training and research.
It recommended that the clergy of each Church should receive
a part of their training from a member of the other Church and
that there should be "collaboration in projects and institutions
of theological scholarship."

As we have already indicated, some of these proposals have
already been put into practice. This is especially true with regard
to cooperation in liturgical revision, theological education, and
relations between religious orders. Retreats involving the two
Churches have become much more common. However, very little
progress has generally been made with most of the other suggestions, at least in Britain. In other words, the two Churches
have not yet reached the "second stage in growing together"
which the Malta Report proposed. In the meantime, however,
the work of the Anglican-Roman Catholic International Commission has bypassed the proposed stage and taken the Churches
some distance beyond it.

In practice, ARCIC, when it came into being in 1970, despite
the very wide terms of reference suggested for it by the Malta

Report, concentrated increasingly on theological questions leaving to others the consideration of the "matters of practical difficulty" of which Pope Paul VI and Dr. Ramsey had spoken. This came about partly because the members of the Commission being mostly professional theologians were best equipped to deal with the doctrinal matters, partly because time was scarcely available for other work. An attempt was made to investigate the "non-theological factors" contributing to the divisions between the two Churches and a sociological survey of the subject was commissioned, but for lack of funds, it never got off the ground. Consequently, the general responsibility for relations between the two Churches has reverted to Lambeth and Rome, and to two special Commissions. A Joint Commission on Marriage was already in existence and in 1975 produced a valuable report which investigated some of the problems raised by marriages between Roman Catholics and Anglicans. A second commission was subsequently appointed to consider the ordination of women, though with no tangible results.

Controversial Doctrines

Between 1970 and 1981, ARCIC met for thirteen sessions of about nine days each. Slightly modifying the agenda set it by the Preparatory Commission, it came to see its main task as that of discovering the extent to which the two Churches share a common faith concerning the three fundamental but controversial doctrines of Eucharist, ordained ministry, and authority in the Church (especially that of the Pope). Successive Agreed Statements on these three topics were published between 1971 and 1977. As it published each document, the Commission invited questions, comments, and criticisms in answer to which in 1979 it issued "Elucidations" of the Statements on Eucharist and Ministry. In 1981, having been instructed by Rome and Canterbury to wind up its work, the Commission submitted its Final Report to the Pope and the Archbishop. This included the agreements already published, a second Statement on Authority, Elucidations of the first Statement on that subject, and an Introduction which set out the doctrine of the Church which underlay the Commission's thinking on Eucharist, Ministry, and Authority.

In seeking reconciliation concerning these three topics, ARCIC's main problem was to show that, despite the controversy which was centered on each of them at the time of the Reformation, fundamental agreement was possible. Naturally, the difficulty usually lay in seeking accord between Roman Catholics and the Protestant or Evangelical section of the Anglican Communion; the differences between Roman Catholics and High Church or Anglo-Catholic Anglicans was predictably much narrower. The difficulties occurred in their most acute and basic form in connection with two aspects of the doctrine of the Eucharist, namely, sacrifice and real presence.

The Eucharist as Sacrifice

For the Evangelical, to call the Eucharist a sacrifice would imply that it is regarded as a repetition of the unrepeatable sacrifice of Christ on Calvary, or that Christ's self-offering on the cross was insufficient and needs to be supplemented by the human action of celebrating the Mass. The Commission believed that it helped to solve this difficulty if one refrained from applying the emotion-charged word "sacrifice" to the Eucharist and spoke instead of a "memorial" or "commemoration" of Christ's saving action, as he himself had commanded his disciples to "do this in commemoration of me." A memorial in this sense is much more than a mere reminder, like the photograph of a friend; it involves a movement downwards from God to man and upwards from man to God. In the movement from God to man, the Eucharist is a memorial insofar as it makes Christ's past sacrifice on the cross effective for the Church in the present. This had been one of the ways in which St. Thomas Aquinas had explained the sense in which Christ is immolated in the Mass. The Commission also saw in the Eucharist an ascending movement from man to God in three senses. First, through the Eucharist, which means "thanksgiving," the Church offers up thanks to God for all his gifts, especially for the saving work of Christ. Secondly, the faithful hold Christ's self-offering up to the Father in supplication. In the words of the Report, they "entreat the benefits of his passion." Thirdly, the faithful "enter into the movement of his self-offering," a phrase which seemed to the Roman Catholic members to express the traditional Catholic belief that the Church is offered to the Father in and with Christ. The Evangelical members, in their turn, recognized that their concern for the unrepeatable nature of the sacrifice of the cross had been met.

The Real Presence of Christ

A similar effort to seek the agreement which was obscured by centuries of controversy also proved successful when applied to the doctrine of the real presence of Christ in the Eucharist. Evangelicals generally suspect that the Catholic doctrine of transsubstantiation implies an almost magical transformation on the physical level of one set of material substances into another. For them, if one is to speak of Christ's presence in the Eucharist, it must be seen as a personal, active presence; he is not present in a material way, like the bread and the wine. Moreover, they stress Christ's presence throughout the entire Eucharistic action not only under the forms of bread and wine but also in the congregation, in the ordained minister, and in the proclamation of the Word of God. All of this arouses among Roman Catholics the counter-suspicion that, for Anglicans, Christ's presence in the Eucharist is merely "subjective," that is, that it is created by the faith of the communicant.

The Commission's attempt to uncover agreement took two directions. To meet the Evangelicals' point, it emphasized the personal, dynamic nature of the Eucharistic presence. To meet the Catholic request that a subjective interpretation of the presence should be excluded, the Commission spoke of two "movements" in the Eucharist. The first movement, which is a gift of God and independent of the individual's faith, is that by which Christ freely makes his sacramental body and blood present as an offering to believers, awaiting their welcome. The second movement is that of the believer who meets Christ's offer of himself with faith, so that "a life-giving encounter results."

Ordained Ministry

Space is not available here for an exposition of the rest of the Final Report at a similar depth. The Statement on Ministry saw the ordained minister as a God-given focus of leadership and unity, who performs this function by proclaiming God's word, leading the people in worship, particularly in the Eucharist, and in giving pastoral guidance. The first Statement on Authority found agreement in basing the authority of Scripture and the authority of the ordained minister on the authority of Christ. With regard to the authority of the ministry, the Commission saw it was essential to the Church Christ founded that the local Church should be equipped with the authority of an ordained minister (the bishop) to focus its Christian life; so too, a similar authority of a universal primate (the Pope) is needed "if God's will for the unity in love and truth of the whole Christian community is to be fulfilled." Nevertheless, there remained Anglican problems concerning the papacy which were discussed in the second document on Authority and which will be considered in the next chapter.

For much of its work, the Commission claimed to have achieved "substantial agreement" among its members. The meaning of this term, namely, agreement over essentials without ruling out a diversity of expression, was explained in Chapter 3. ARCIC claimed substantial agreement in this sense for its conclusions on the Eucharist and Ministry. Because of the remaining problems concerning the papacy, it did not claim substantial agreement for the two documents on Authority, though it might reasonably have done so for most of its teaching on the subject. It does, however, speak more modestly of a "convergence," such that "substantial agreement . . . is now possible."

Commission Without Teaching Authority

Although ARCIC is a body established by the Pope and the Archbishop of Canterbury, it has no official teaching authority. Hence its findings will not constitute an agreement between the two Churches until it has been formally ratified by each of them. Since the publication of the Final Report in 1982, it has been subjected to close scrutiny at every level: at regional, diocesan, and even lower levels. On the Catholic side, the Vatican Congregation for the Doctrine of the Faith in 1982 issued preliminary *Observations* intended to provide guidance for the continuation of the dialogue. The final verdict, however, must take a very different form in each of the two Churches. The Anglican Church is not, strictly speaking, a single Church but a Communion of twenty-seven Churches or provinces, each of which is self-governing. Although there are various bodies which have the task of coordinating the whole Anglican Communion, such as the Lambeth Conference of bishops which meets every ten years, the regular meetings of the primates of each of the provinces, and a standing Anglican Consultative Council, these bodies are only advisory. There is no central organ which has power to make decisions which bind the whole Communion. Consequently, whatever endorsement of ARCIC is given by the Lambeth Conference or any other central body may carry great moral weight but will not represent a binding decision until it has been ratified individually by the provinces. The structures of authority in the Roman Catholic Church, by contrast, are strongly centralized. Decisions taken by the Pope and the collegial and curial organization centered on him are binding on the whole Church.

On the Anglican side, a formal resolution concerning ARCIC was taken at the Lambeth Conference of 1988. Resolutions were passed by a large majority endorsing ARCIC's Statements on Eucharist and Ministry as "consonant in substance with the faith of Anglicans. The Authority Statements were also approved, though in a more qualified way, as "a firm basis for the direction and agenda of the continuing dialogue." However, the resolutions called for further exploration of a number of associated issues, such as the ordination of women and "the concept of a universal primacy."

The Roman Catholic response, on the other hand, as I write this in February 1989, had not yet been published.

ARCIC II Established

When the two Churches have each completed their separate responses to ARCIC I, it seems desirable that these responses provide the basis for a common declaration of faith concerning Eucharist, ministry, and authority, thus inaugurating a further new stage in their relationship. Meanwhile, a further step has already been inaugurated. Shortly after the publication of ARCIC I's Final Report in 1982, Pope John Paul II and Archbishop Robert Runcie met in Canterbury and issued a Common Declaration in which they declared "the next stage of our common pilgrimage in faith and hope towards the unity for which we long." Accordingly, they announced the establishment of a new Commission (ARCIC II) to replace the original one which on the completion of its report had ceased to exist. The Pope and the Archbishop set out the agenda for the new body under three heads. The first item was the examination of remaining doctrinal differences which divide the two Churches; the second, the obstacles in the way of the mutual recognition of ministries; the third, the "practical steps" which "will be necessary when [N.B. *when* not *if*!], on the basis of our unity in faith, we are able to proceed to the restoration of full communion."

Justification by Faith

The work at this stage has been proceeding steadily. Taking up the first item on the agenda, the new Commission heeded the repeated requests of Evangelicals for the examination of the doctrine of justification by faith which had featured so importantly in the reformation debates and which still holds a central position in the faith and devotion of many Protestants. The Commission published its Agreed Statement on this subject in 1987 under the title *Salvation and the Church*. Since then, it is being submitted to a similar process of examination as the work of ARCIC I. The 1988 Lambeth Conference spoke of it as "a timely and significant contribution to the understanding of the Churches' doctrine of salvation." The Congregation for the Doctrine of the Faith also in the same year issued its *Observations*, which contrast interestingly with their *Observations* of 1982. In each document, the Congregation acknowledges that ARCIC has achieved a significant agreement; in 1987, indeed the commendation is more generous. In both cases, however, they judge that traditional Catholic teaching has not been expressed clearly enough to remove the risk of ambiguity. One important difference, however, between the two statements by the CDF is that the new document gives sympathetic, though critical, attention to the method which ARCIC adopted of avoiding polemical language, admitting that truths can be expressed in a variety of ways and seeking substantial agreement underlying different formulations. An official commentary on the *Observations* disclaims any intention of "disavowing anything in a method [i.e. the method employed by ARCIC] which has produced incontestable results." Nevertheless, the Congregation would wish this method to be supplemented by "a rigorous comparison between the respective positions" of the two Churches.

Tangible Results

In this chapter, we have had much to say about new steps and stages. Almost all the progress so far discussed, however, has concerned agreements on paper. But one gets the impression that the ordinary faithful of the two Churches who desire unity have a healthy scepticism about ecumenical talks and agreements which make no practical difference to the life of the Churches. Ecumenical agreement should be good news; it should get off the paper into the minds and hearts and lives of Christian people. It was with the desire of such tangible results that ARCIC I wrote:

> The convergence reflected in our Final Report would appear to call for the establishing of a new relationship between our Churches as a next stage in the journey towards Christian unity. . . . There are high expectations that significant initiatives will be boldly undertaken to deepen our reconciliation and lead us forward in the quest for the full communion to which we have been committed, in obedience to God, from the beginning of our dialogue.

Having completed its work on justification, ARCIC II has turned its attention to practical steps and, as I write, is working on a document which bears the provisional title *Growth in Communion.*

Duty of Mutual Trust

ARCIC's recommendation of new practical steps based on growing doctrinal agreement is not without problems. What is required is official agreement between the two Churches and not simply agreement reached by the members of ecumenical commissions. However, even after each Church has completed its official judgment on ARCIC's work, there will remain the problem of comparing the two responses. The CDF's *Observations* have indicated the difficulties and risk of ambiguity involved in this process. Will a new commission have to agree about the amount of agreement revealed by the two Churches' responses? One is close to demanding an infinite process of dialogue and reception. To break out of this endless circle, it will be necessary at some point for each of the Churches to pass from assertions of its own faith to a profession of trust in the faith of the other. If the Churches have indeed a duty to unite, such a leap of trust will be not an act of weakness but a duty. After all, many human decisions, as Newman saw, have to be made on the basis not of absolute certainty but of a convergence of probabilities. This is always true whenever human beings are called upon to trust one another. My certainty of a person's trustworthiness will be based on a series of experiences, none of which by itself gives adequate proof but which, taken together, provide completely reliable grounds for trust. In the same way, there may come a point in the relationship between two Churches when intellectual examination of one another's faith and practice has achieved all it can achieve and must now be succeeded by trust—not a blind trust, but one that has its justification in a deep and gradually acquired familiarity with one another's faith and practice.

Duty to Act

It is not only at the end of the process, when the time comes for the Churches to decide whether they are justified in uniting, that such a leap of trust is called for. There will be many points along the line at which each Church will have to ask itself what new step towards unity is justifiable and indeed obligatory on the basis of the incomplete evidence for agreement in faith currently available. Accordingly, the question we have to ask at the present stage of the process is this: on the ground of the growing doctrinal consensus between the two Churches, even if the precise extent of that consensus cannot yet be established, what practical steps towards reunion are they justified in taking now? Or, rather, a significantly different question should be asked: what steps have the Churches a *duty* to take now in the light of not only growing consensus but the obligation to seek reunion? As Pope John Paul II said at an Orthodox liturgy in Constantinople in 1979:

> We must not be afraid to reconsider, on both sides, and in consultation with one another, canonical rules established when our awareness of our communion . . . was still dimmed, rules which, perhaps, no longer correspond to the results of the dialogue of charity and to possibilities they have opened. It is important in order that the faithful on both sides realize the progress that has been made.

Ordination of Women as Bishops

The time I am writing these words is one when such easily recognizable changes are especially needed so as to overcome a widespread mood of ecumenical despair. The Lambeth Conference of 1988, encouraging though it was to ARCIC's work, had already accentuated this feeling of pessimism in many quarters through its resolution that each province should "respect the decision and attitudes of other provinces in the ordination and consecration of women to the episcopate"; and in February 1989, as a sequel to this resolution, the first woman bishop was consecrated in the United States. The difficulty this chain of events has caused is twofold. First, the ordination of women as bishops creates greater problems than their ordination as priests, not only because bishops bear a greater responsibility for the unity of the Church but also because rejection of women bishops involves the rejection of any priests they ordain, male as well as female, so that the Roman Catholic recognition of Anglican orders is made correspondingly more remote. Secondly, the issue has highlighted the absence of any body with the power to make decisions binding upon the whole Anglican Communion and has led many Anglicans to conclude that its internal communion has been "impaired." For reasons such as these, Pope John Paul II, in his 1988 end-of-the-year speech to the Vatican Curia, took the unusual step of publicly criticizing another Church and spoke of the decision taken at Lambeth as a "shadow" on the year, which "did not adequately take into account either the ecumenical or ecclesiastical dimensions of the problem," and impeded the success of the work of ARCIC. He asked the Archbishop of Canterbury to "make every effort so that the painful consequences may be avoided, not only in ecumenical relations but within the Anglican community." Some Anglicans will regretfully judge that it was right for the prospects of reunion with Rome to take second place to the correction of what they see as a ministry made defective by the exclusion of women. Nevertheless, the decision emphasized a second ecumenical problem, namely, the difficulty for Roman Catholics of entering into agreement with a Church which feels bound to "respect" any dissenting voice raised by individual provinces.

But precisely because of these difficulties and the prevalent mood of defeatism, there is all the more reason to find some new and significant step forward which will show that Christ's will for the unity of his followers is not doomed to frustration. If the mutual recognition of orders and even limited intercommunion are ruled out for the time being by the events of 1988 and 1989, there is urgent need for us to devise some more modest measure.

Perhaps the very fragmentation of Anglican decision-making which has been described above can be turned to a source of hope. The best hope for significant practical initiatives seems to lie in local and national arrangements. What is feasible and desirable in one place may not be so in another. It might even be possible that, where an Anglican province has decided against women priests, perhaps in such provinces an acceptable way could even be found, along the lines suggested in Chapter 4, for Roman Catholic uncertainties concerning Anglican orders to be removed, without driving a wedge between such a province and the rest of the Anglican Ministry.

Moving Forward Is a Duty

One thing is certain, as has been often said already in this chapter: the search for some significant step forward is not an option which we are free to decline. Even if we can see no prospect of success, we would do well to remember, as we work out our ecumenical salvation in fear and trembling, that it is God's power which is at work in all our efforts (cf. Phil 2:12-13).

Chapter 6

REMAINING PROBLEMS

In this chapter, I shall discuss four problems which have frequently emerged in the discussions between Roman Catholics and Anglicans and which are also pertinent to the former Church's relations with other bodies.

The Papacy

Pope Paul VI spent more than a year in the preparation of his first encyclical *Ecclesiam Suam* (1964). Its third section, which concerns dialogue, is of great ecumenical interest. In the course of a discussion of the difficulty which many Christians have in accepting the prerogatives of the Roman Catholic Church, the Pope made the following sad observation:

> It fills our heart with sorrow that many brothers separated from communion with the Apostolic See think that we ourselves, while supporting the idea of reconciliation, are actually an obstacle to it. . . . Do not some people say that, if the primacy of the Bishop of Rome were abolished, it would be easier for the separated Churches to be united with the Catholic Church in a single body?

Addressing the Secretariat for Christian Unity in 1967, Pope Paul VI repeated this opinion in an even more shocking form:

> The Pope, as we well know, is undoubtedly the gravest obstacle in the path of ecumenism.

INTERPRETATION OF PAPAL PRIMACY

However, far from being a scandal, the Pope maintained, the papacy, if properly understood,

> is like the main hinge of the Church . . . not a supreme authority puffed up with spiritual pride or eager for human domination, but a primacy of service, ministration and love . . . the indispensable principle of truth, charity and unity, a pastoral mission of guidance, of service and of brotherhood.

In the past, it was not uncommon to hear ecumenically minded Anglicans and others affirm that they could consider accepting a papal primacy provided it was not a primacy of jurisdiction, defined in terms of power but a primacy of honor. This concession, though generous, is surely inappropriate, as Christians who claim to be disciples of the Master who "humbled himself and became obedient unto death" (Phil 2:8) can hardly wish a primate's position to be defined in terms of honor. Cardinal Joseph Ratzinger must be closer to the mark in suggesting that the primacy is to be understood rather in "martyrological" terms as a primacy of sacrifice in the sharing of Christ's cross. Pope Paul VI more than once indicated that his primacy was a primacy of love for the whole Church, quoting the phrase of St. Ignatius of Antioch, "presiding over the universal assembly of love." The present Archbishop of Canterbury gave favorable consideration to a papacy of this type in his opening address at the 1988 Lambeth Conference. Since "the Son of Man also came not to be served but to serve" (Mark 10:45) and since the Pope has traditionally been given the title "Servant of the servants of God," perhaps the best definition of papal primacy is that given in *Ecclesiam Suam*, a "primacy of service." In the same vein, ARCIC I spoke of the primacy of the Bishop of Rome as

> not an autocratic power over the Church but a service in and to the Church which is a communion in faith and charity of local churches.

The papacy exists to serve the Church. The papacy should not diminish the authority of individual bishops but underpin it.

These principles are already implied in the definition of papal primacy at Vatican I in 1870. The purpose of the Petrine authority is "that the episcopate itself should be one and undivided":

> So far is this power of the Supreme Pontiff from weakening the ordinary and immediate power of episcopal jurisdiction . . . that the latter is asserted, strengthened, and vindicated by the supreme and universal pastor.

Pope Paul VI acknowledged this principle in his 1967 address to the Secretariat for Christian Unity in which he stated that the papacy was

> intended to be . . . a pastoral mission of guidance, of service, and of brotherhood which does not challenge the liberty and honor of anyone who has a legitimate position in the Church of God, but instead protects the rights of all and demands no other obedience than that which is demanded from the sons of a family.

Function of All Primacy

This understanding of the papal office serving the Church by supporting and unifying the authority of all the bishops throughout the world is shared by ARCIC I. The Commission affirmed that the function of all primacy, whether the universal primacy of the Pope, the primacy exercised by the leading bishop in a particular region, or primacy within a worldwide body like the Anglican Communion, is to

> foster the *koinonia* by helping the bishops in their task of apostolic leadership both in their local Church and in the Church universal. . . . [A primate's] intervention in the affairs of a local Church should not be made in such a way as to usurp the responsibility of its bishop.

The authority of the universal primate does not

> undermine that of the metropolitan or diocesan bishop. Primacy is not an autocratic power over the Church but a service in and to the Church which is a communion in faith and charity of local Churches.

In fact, all ordained ministry in the Church (ARCIC sometimes uses the Greek word *episcope* in this connection) exists to help Christians to follow Christ freely. The obedience which is due to the bishop does not diminish the freedom and love with which each Christian is called to serve God:

> It is the responsibility of those exercising episcope to enable all the people to use the gifts of the Spirit which they have received for the enrichment of the Church's common life.

This principle is sometimes described in terms borrowed from social ethics as the principle of subsidiarity. It was enunciated within that context in 1931 by Pope Pius XI in his encyclical *Quadragesimo Anno:*

> It is an injustice, a grave evil, and a disturbance of right order for a larger and higher organization to arrogate to itself functions which can be performed efficiently by smaller and lower bodies. . . . The true aim of all social activity should be to help individual members of the social body, but never to destroy or absorb them.

The next Pope, Pius XII, recognized that the principle of subsidiarity applied also to "the life of the Church, without prejudice to its hierarchical structure"; he did not, however, work out the principle's ecclesial implications.

PRIMACY, NOT DESPOTISM

Thus, in agreeing to the need of a universal primacy for the sake of the unity of the Church, ARCIC was not giving a blank check to an absolute papal despotism.

What the Commission said, in a careful and technical formulation, which corresponds closely with the teaching of Vatican II on collegiality, was that

> this general pattern of the complementary primatial and conciliar aspects of episcope serving the *koinonia* of the Churches needs to be realized at the universal level.

However, Roman Catholics cannot expect other Christians to accept the papacy until it is shown in practice to respect the authority of local Churches and their bishops or, in other words, to respect the principle of subsidiarity. It is not difficult to see how the visits of Pope John Paul II can be a source of strength especially to hard-pressed sections of the Church throughout the world; other Churches have found themselves needing to develop a similar office of leadership. The World Council of Churches is represented round the world by its Secretary General, while the Archbishop of Canterbury finds himself in countries like South Africa forced against his will to adopt something of the role of an Anglican pope in supporting the local Church.

NEED FOR BALANCED, UNIVERSAL AUTHORITY

But on the other hand, the papacy can present the appearance of an overcentralized and repressive authority. Consequently, in the words of Garrett Sweeney, "the Primacy can never become credible until its limits are defined." The first statement on Authority of ARCIC I was alive to this danger:

> Although primacy and conciliarity are complementary elements of *episcope* it has often happened that one has been emphasized at the expense of the other, even to the point of serious imbalance. When Churches have been separated from one another, this danger has been increased. The *koinonia* of the Churches requires that a proper balance be preserved between the two with the responsible participation of the whole people of God.

It is accordingly important that such a balance should be reached in the resolution of the current debate in the Roman Catholic Church about the authority of regional episcopal conferences.

It is also vital that Rome's choice of bishops should not give reasonable grounds for the feeling that

> legitimate local aspirations and needs are being overlooked.

FOUR REMAINING PROBLEMS

At the end of the first statement on Authority, after affirming the need for a balanced universal primacy, ARCIC I felt it necessary to list four remaining Anglican problems concerning the papacy: its basis in Scripture, the assertion by Vatican I that the papacy exists by divine law (*ex iure divino*), papal infallibility, and papal jurisdiction. Despite these problems, the Commission could speak of a "significant convergence." The Commission returned to these four problems in the second Statement on Authority, and reached agreement on all except infallibility.

The question of infallibility concerns the means by which Christ's promise that the Holy Spirit would guide the Church into all the truth is fulfilled (John 16:13). Both sides concurred that popes have at times in the past been God's agents for preserving the Church from error. The Anglican members, however, stated that they could not take it as certain that a definition promulgated by the Pope was a matter of binding faith before the Church as a whole had had time after reflection to recognize that the definition was faithful to the truth of the Gospel. This process of reflection is often called "reception." For Roman Catholics, on the other hand, if a papal definition has fulfilled the conditions which were laid down in the Vatican I decree, it is at once acknowledged to be free from error. However, even for Roman Catholics, the process of reception of a definition is important, if it is to be assimilated into the life and prayer of the Church. Sometimes, too, such reception may help to confirm the truth of the definition and clarify its meaning. For these reasons, it seemed to the Commission that with regard to the papacy, and even papal infallibility, "substantial agreements are . . . now possible."

The Blessed Virgin Mary

ARCIC I, in setting out the Anglican problems concerning infallibility, stated that

> special difficulties are created by the recent Marian dogmas [i.e., the Immaculate Conception and the Assumption], because Anglicans doubt the appropriateness, or even the possibility, of defining them as essential to the faith of believers.

The response of the Episcopal Church of the United States to ARCIC distinguished two sides to this difficulty: agreement needs to be reached not only about the content of the Marian doctrines, which some Anglicans already accept, but also about their status as binding dogmas.

In fact, the ARCIC report contains a surprisingly wide agreement concerning the Blessed Virgin: "Anglicans and Roman Catholics can agree in much of the truth that these two dogmas are designed to affirm." Eight points of agreement are set out:

> 1. Marian doctrine does not contradict the fact that her Son is the One mediator.
>
> 2. Marian doctrine is "inseparably linked with the doctrines of Christ and the Church."
>
> 3. The Commission is agreed in recognizing her "unique grace and vocation."
>
> 4. Both Churches include Marian feasts in their calendars, "according to her honor in the communion of saints."
>
> 5. Mary was "prepared by divine grace to be the mother of our Redeemer."
>
> 6. She was herself "redeemed and received into glory."
>
> 7. She is "a model of holiness, obedience, and faith for all Christians."
>
> 8. "It is possible to regard her as a prophetic figure of the Church."

CLARIFYING ROMAN CATHOLIC STATEMENTS

Before asking how far this agreement answers the two questions raised by the American Anglican comment, it will be useful to consider three recent Roman Catholic statements which clarify the interpretation of Marian doctrine. First, the Vatican II Decree on the Church, *Lumen Gentium*, reaffirms the ancient teaching that Mary is the "type and outstanding model in faith and charity" of the Church (53). Doctrine about Mary never concerns her simply as an individual but always expresses the way in which she uniquely realizes some aspect of the Church. Mariology is ecclesiology. Secondly, Paul VI in 1974 in his Exhortation on devotion to Mary entitled *Marialis Cultus* affirmed that "in the Virgin Mary everything is relative to Christ and dependent upon him" (25). Mariology is Christology. Thirdly, the same document states that Marian devotion should have a "biblical imprint" (30). Mariology is biblical theology.

We shall go a long way towards answering the first American Anglican question which concerns the *content* of the two Marian dogmas if we can interpret them in these three ways and show that such an interpretation can claim official approval. The dogma of the Immaculate Conception has a clear Christological dimension as it teaches that it was by an anticipation of Christ's redeeming work that Mary was preserved from original sin. *Lumen Gentium* adds that she was "enriched by God with gifts appropriate" to the role of mother of God, the Son made man (56). The same decree of Vatican II indicates the ecclesiological and biblical dimensions of the dogma:

> In the most Blessed Virgin Mary the Church has already reached that perfection whereby she exists without spot or wrinkle (cf. Eph 5:27) (65).

It is *Marialis Cultus* which most clearly gives the dogma of the Assumption of Mary the same three connections, namely with Christ, the Church, and the Bible. The feast of the Assumption

> sets before the eyes of the Church and of all mankind the image and the consoling proof of the fulfillment of their final hope, namely, that this full glorification is the destiny of all those whom Christ has made his brothers, having "flesh and blood in common with them" (Heb 2:14; cf. Gal 4:4) (6).

HIERARCHY OF TRUTHS

It still remains to answer the second question raised by the American Anglicans, namely, whether the dogmas are central enough to be articles of faith. The "hierarchy of truths" propounded by the Decree on Ecumenism of Vatican II suggests an answer:

> When comparing doctrines with one another, they should remember that in Catholic doctrine there exists an order or "hierarchy"

of truths, since they vary in their relation to the foundation of the Christian faith.

Many different interpretations have been given of this passage which was inserted into the text of the decree at a late stage without a clear explanation being given. I suggested in Chapter 3 that the meaning is that the foundation of Christian faith consists of dogmas which are formulated explicitly in terms of the saving work of the threefold God through the incarnate Son. The "lower" levels in the hierarchy of truths are occupied by dogmas which are connected with the "higher" dogmas of God, Christ, and salvation *by implication,* though not stated *explicitly* in these terms. Marian dogmas are definable because they are definitions, in terms of Mary, of some truth or truths concerning Jesus Christ and his saving work.

The ARCIC Agreement itself indicated how for Roman Catholics these two Marian dogmas are applications of the fundamental Christian doctrines concerning salvation:

> The affirmation of the Roman Catholic Church that Mary was conceived without original sin [i.e., the dogma of the Immaculate Conception] is based on recognition of her unique role within the mystery of the Incarnation. By being thus prepared to be the mother of our Redeemer, she also becomes a sign that the salvation won by Christ was operative among all mankind before his birth. The affirmation that her glory in heaven involves full participation in the fruits of salvation [i.e., the dogma of the Assumption] expresses and reinforces our faith that the life of the world to come has already broken into the life of our world.

One could add that by teaching that Mary was received into heaven with her body as well as her soul, the Church emphasizes that we are not saved by escape from the body, but it is our whole embodied human existence which enters into glory.

Is Unity in Faith Possible?

There remains, however, a further question. Is unity in faith possible between those who hold the Marian applications of the foundation of faith to be definable and those who do not? Clearly, no such unity would be possible between those who profess faith in these foundational doctrines themselves and those who do not. Nor would there be unity in faith between Roman Catholics, who hold the Marian dogmas to be articles of faith, and others who hold them to be false or even heretical. But Roman Catholics could, I suggest, enjoy a genuine unity in faith with Anglicans who accept that the Marian dogmas were at least legitimate interpretations of the foundational truths even if they were not themselves able to give to the Marian applications an assent of faith.

Purgatory and Indulgences

The first Agreed Statement published by ARCIC II, *Salvation and the Church*, concluded:

> We are agreed that this is not an area where any remaining differences of theological interpretation or ecclesiological emphasis, either within or between our Communions, can justify our continued separation (n. 32).

ARCIC I would probably have said that "substantial agreement" had been established, with the understanding that there could remain "a divergence in matters of practice and in theological judgments relating to them, without destroying a common . . . faith."

There does in fact remain a measure of such divergence in matters relating to salvation and the Church. Another ecumenical Commission, the United States Lutheran-Roman Catholic dialogue group, although, like ARCIC, reaching fundamental agreement on the doctrine of justification by faith, nevertheless set out some areas in which consensus had not yet been attained. These included:

> traditionally disputed doctrines such as the sacrament of penance, Masses for special intentions, indulgences, and purgatory.

The problem is this. Roman Catholics believe that a person may die in a state of grace but still need to pass through the purifying experience of purgatory before being admitted to heaven.

They also believe that the prayers and good works of the Church can assist the dead in this process of purification, and that the Church has the power to attach to these pious acts an indulgence or declaration that they are of benefit to the departed who are undergoing the purifying process of purgatory. How then can Roman Catholics maintain at the same time that the restoration of the sinner to grace is wholly the work of God through the merits of Jesus Christ? Do the Roman Catholic doctrines of purgatory and indulgences not imply that Christ did not do everything that needed to be done on our behalf, leaving something for the Church to add to his redeeming work?

ARCIC was of course aware of the problem, and made more than one attempt to draft a section on such topics to be included in "Salvation and the Church." Finally, in order not to obscure the main lines of the document and to avoid holding up the completion of the text, the Commission decided to reserve its comments on the subject for another time, while including a paragraph which would alert the careful reader to the issues and hint at a solution. All Christians, both living and dead, the Commission stated, are "bound together in a communion of prayer"; the act of pronouncing forgiveness in the name of Christ is an example of this bond of prayer:

> The Church may also help them [repentant sinners] to a deeper realization of the mercy of God by asking for practical amends for what has been done amiss. Such penitential disciplines, and other devotional practices, are not in any way intended to put God under obligation. Rather, they provide a form in which one may more fully embrace the free mercy of God.

NEED FOR PURIFICATION

Underlying these words is the conviction that in the process of justification, human beings are not simply passive. It is a sound instinct in the repentant sinner to wish to "make amends" for his faults, without implying that forgiveness is anything but a free gift of God. The doctrine of purgatory states that even after we are forgiven, there remain in our personalities the traces of sin, the engrained harm which sin does to our psyche, which have to be purified before we can enter into the joy of the Lord in heaven. There is a close connection between this teaching and that of St. John:

> We know that when he appears we shall be like him, for we shall see him as he is. And everyone who thus hopes in him purifies himself as he is pure (1 John 3:23).

Where this purification is not completed in this life, it has to be completed in the next. However, it has not been revealed to us what form this purification takes nor whether it is instantaneous or has a duration; traditional language about purgatorial fires is symbolic. The Council of Trent contented itself with stating baldly that "purgatory exists, and the souls detained there are helped by the suffrages of the faithful," while forbidding subtle speculation on the subject in popular sermons.

It is not only the individual sinner who is called to cooperate in the process of justification. Belief that the sinner is justified by grace alone (*sola gratia*, as the Reformers saw so clearly) does not exclude the belief that God uses human instruments, who derive all their efficacy from God. It was to make this point that ARCIC II chose for its statement on justification the title "Salvation and the Church"; God calls and empowers the Church to be the sign, steward, instrument, and sacrament of God's saving work. The doctrine of indulgences, as applied to the souls in purgatory, is based on the belief that the departed are aided in their purgatorial process by the prayers and good works of the Church on earth. This sharing between the living and the dead is a consequence of the communion of saints.

The most complete and authoritative exposition of the doctrine of indulgences is contained in Paul VI's Constitution *Indulgentiarum Doctrina*.

The Ordination of Women

When ARCIC first met in 1970, no part of the Anglican Communion was ordaining women to the priesthood. It is true that one of the provinces, Hong Kong, had felt justified in ordaining a small number of women during the second World War, when there was an acute shortage of clergy, but out of deference to the reactions of the other Anglican provinces, these women had ceased to exercise their presbyterate.

Consequently, when the Commission formulated its Agreed Statement on Ministry and Ordination in 1973, it saw no need to make any reference to the question whether the class of people who can be ordained to ministry might include women. Even when shortly afterwards a group of retired bishops in the United States did ordain some women priests, the rest of the American episcopate repudiated their action as invalid.

REASON FOR ANGLICAN OBJECTION

The situation was soon to change. The rejection of the ordained women by the American bishops was not based on the judgment that in principle only males can be ordained; the reason was that the ordaining bishops had behaved schismatically in acting without the consent of the whole episcopal body. Before long, however, the American bishops were to accept the principle that female gender was no bar to ordination; at the time of writing, about six Anglican provinces have women priests, including the United States, Canada, and New Zealand. None of the British provinces has yet taken that step, though England, Wales, and Scotland have women deacons. Legislation providing for the ordination of women priests is in the pipeline in England, but at the moment it seems by no means certain that when it comes to the final vote it will receive the necessary two-thirds majority in General Synod.

The Roman Catholic Church has never varied in its judgment that only men can be priests. It is sometimes suggested that the question has never been faced until modern times, but that is not true. In its early days, faced with sects which had female priests, the Church rejected on principle the practice of ordaining women. It is certain that in the first centuries the Church made frequent use of deaconesses or women deacons, especially for the sake of decency in connection with the total immersion and anointing of women at baptism, but whether they were ordained in the strict sense is a matter of dispute among scholars.

ROMAN CATHOLIC OBJECTIONS TO ORDAINING WOMEN

However, although the Church seems to have been unwavering in rejecting a female priesthood, the reasons alleged for that rejection sometimes owe much to contemporary cultural conditions. Thus St. Thomas Aquinas argues that a woman necessarily holds a place of subjection (*statum subjectionis habet*), and therefore cannot receive the sacrament of order as it confers a position of superiority. His argument does not, however, depend as completely as at first sight it appears to do on a social situation which can scarcely be thought to obtain in the age of Margaret Thatcher. Aquinas recognized that in the past, and even in his own day, women could hold civil power (*temporaliter dominari*). He presumably therefore based his reasoning on an understanding of female sexuality and psychology, rather than on the political and social realities of his day.

The fullest official Roman Catholic statement of the case against the ordination of women is a Declaration published by the Congregation for the Doctrine of the Faith in 1976 entitled *Inter Insigniores*. This document weaved a number of considerations together to show that the Church's unbroken refusal to accept women as priests was fundamentally due not to cultural factors, but to the respective symbolism of male and female gender. The male is the natural symbol for Christ the Bridegroom as the female is for the Church, Christ's Bride:

> In actions which demand the character of ordination and in which Christ himself, the author of the Covenant, the Bridegroom and Head of the Church, is represented, exercising his ministry of salvation which is in the highest degree the case of the Eucharist, his role (this is the original sense of the word *persona*) must be taken by a man. This does not stem from any personal superiority of the latter in the order of values, but only from a difference of fact on the level of functions and service.

Without going so far as to say that the maleness of ordained ministry is a revealed doctrine, the Congregation states that the ordination of women is not a possibility:

> The Church, in fidelity to the example of the Lord, does not consider herself authorized to admit women to priestly ordination. . . . The Catholic Church has never felt that priestly or episcopal ordination can be validly conferred on women.

It may be of some ecumenical significance that the condemnation does not appear to apply to women deacons.

Pope John Paul II endorsed the CDF's argument in his Letter on the dignity and vocation of women entitled *Mulieris Dignitatem* (August 1988). In the Eucharist, Christ is united with his body the Church as the Bridegroom to the Bride. "It is legitimate to conclude" that the reason why Christ "linked it [the Eucharist] in such an explicit way to the priestly service of the Apostles," all of whom were male, was to express the relationship between the masculine and the feminine.

WOMEN AND THE CHURCH'S MISSION

However, to exclude women from priesthood need not involve excluding them from a full part in the Church's mission. Two months before the CDF's Declaration was published in 1976, another Vatican Congregation also produced a document on women, this time on "The Role of Women in Evangelization." Similarly, Pope John Paul's assertion of a male ministry makes up only a small section of a document about the vocation of women. Men and women, he writes, share "a common responsibility for the destiny of humanity":

> The Church gives thanks for all the manifestations of the female "genius" which have appeared in the course of history, in the midst of all peoples and nations; she gives thanks for all the charisms which the Holy Spirit distributes to women in the history of the People of God, for all the victories which she owes to their faith, hope, and charity.

Mulieris Dignitatem was followed before the end of the year by the Exhortation *Christifideles Laici* in which Pope John Paul reflected on the conclusions of the 1987 Synod of Bishops concerning the vocation and mission of the laity. The Pope affirms with the Synod that one can understand woman's role and function in society only by turning the discussion to the more fundamental question of what concerns her "meaning as a person." Men and women are fundamentally equal but different and complementary. Woman's potentiality for motherhood gives her a specific sensitivity towards the human person and all that constitutes the individual's true welfare, beginning with the fundamental value of life.

From this, it follows that

> women have the task of assuring the moral dimension of culture, the dimension, namely, of a culture worthy of the person.

This is all the more important in the present age,

> when the development of science and technology is not always inspired and measured by true wisdom, with the inevitable risk of "dehumanizing" human life.

This understanding of the female contribution to social life applies to the Church as well as to secular society. The Pope endorses the Synod's affirmation that

> without discrimination women should be participants in the life of the Church, and also in consultation and the process of coming to decisions.

The fact that women cannot be priests implies a difference not of "dignity and holiness" but of "function."

WOMEN'S INCREASED RESPONSIBILITY IN THE CHURCH

Although the Catholic Church still has a long way to go before harnessing to the Church's mission the full potentiality of the female charisms, women have in recent years been called upon to play a much more responsible part. Liturgically, in many parishes, they are numbered among the readers and auxiliary

ministers of Holy Communion. Their gifts are much more frequently used in spiritual direction and retreat-giving, and in pastoral care of the aged and the sick. The number of qualified
women theologians has greatly increased. Is it possible that in
time the Church will come to recognize their vocation by giving
them a particular place within the hierarchical structure of the
Church, if not as priests, by some other kind of formal, or even
sacramental, commissioning or ordination? But even then, how
would full communion, or even limited intercommunion, be possible between Churches, one of which believed that women could
and should be priests, the other that maleness is essential to Christian priesthood?

These four problems have been discussed from the point of
view of relations between the Roman Catholic and Anglican
Churches. It is important, however, to widen one's horizon and
consider how they appear to Orthodox eyes.

How the Orthodox View Ecumenical Problems

The Orthodox retain long memories of the ill-treatment or
proselytizing which they experienced at the hands of the Roman
Catholic Church. They are accordingly even less predisposed to
accepting the papacy than the Anglicans. While recognizing the
Bishop of Rome as the Patriarch of the West, they see no reason
for submitting to his jurisdiction. Even the Patriarch of Constantinople, Athenagoras, who related so constructively with Pope
Paul VI, stopped short of conceding a primacy of jurisdiction to
the Pope, while allowing that the Bishop of Rome was "the first
in honor among us, 'he who presides in charity.' "[3]

Such limits to the allowances which even the most friendly
Orthodox feel justified in making to the papacy have led Roman
Catholic ecumenists to rethink their position. Without discard-
ing the belief that the Pope has jurisdiction applies to different
parts of the Church in different ways. The Pope's authority as

3. *TAIE*, 70–71; *Tomos Agapis*, Rome-Istanbul 1971, 380–81. The Patriarch was
referring, as we have seen Pope Paul VI himself doing earlier, to the words of
St. Ignatius of Antioch.

bishop of the diocese of Rome is distinct from his authority as primate of the universal Church, and in between these two levels there is his authority as Patriarch of the West. Many of the papal directives with which Roman Catholics today are familiar, such as the insistence that lecturers in theological faculties should have a commission from Rome, come from the Pope as Patriarch of the West and presumably would not apply to the Orthodox Church when it was reunited with Rome. A papacy in a reestablished world Church would necessarily be less interventionist than the papacy with which Roman Catholics are familiar.

On the other hand, the Orthodox position with regard to the other three problems is much closer to the Roman Catholic. The two Churches share a strong devotion to the Mother of God and a faith in her powers of intercession. Although the Orthodox do not support the Roman Catholic action in declaring the Immaculate Conception and the Assumption to be articles of faith, their own belief in Mary's holiness and assumption into heaven have much in common with the Roman Catholic dogmas. Again, while not subscribing to a formal dogma concerning purgatory, the Orthodox, no less than Roman Catholics, believe in the importance of prayer for the dead. With regard to the ordination of women to the priesthood, the Orthodox opposition is even firmer than that of Rome.

Chapter 7

PROSPECTS

What I have written so far on the search for unity has concentrated on relations between Roman Catholics and Anglicans, for, as a member of ARCIC for nearly twenty years, it is to relations between those two Churches that most of my ecumenical efforts have been directed. I have explored in the first six chapters of this book the obligation which Christians have to unite, the type of unity which they should seek, the progressive nature of that search, and finally the obstacles that stand in the way. The difficulty in removing some of those obstacles led us to conclude that the best hope for progress might lie in practical initiatives conducted at the national and local levels rather than in a new relationship between the whole Roman Catholic Church and the whole Anglican Communion.

New Problems

But here new problems arise. The constitutions of the Roman Catholic Church and the Anglican Communion are not symmetrical. The twenty-seven Anglican provinces, while interdependent, are self-governing; the Roman Catholic Church has central as well as regional and local levels of government. If in England the Roman Catholic Church and the Church of England judged it fit to enter into a new formal relationship, the Anglican Communion as a whole would have no power of veto, but the papacy could exercise such a veto if it judged that the unity of the whole Roman Catholic Church was compromised. Moreover, it is far from clear to what extent two Churches could become more closely united without affecting the other Churches with which they were already in communion. If the Church of England, for example, is in communion with the Episcopalian Church in Scotland, could the former Church enter into communion with Rome if it was not yet possible for the Scottish Church to do so? Can A be in communion with both B and C if B and C cannot enter into communion with one another? Would an affirmative answer to this question reduce communion from the level of faith and sacramental life to that of diplomatic relations and administrative convenience? For the Roman Catholic Church, the problem is particularly acute because to be in communion with one part of that Church is to be in communion with the Pope and therefore with the whole Roman Catholic Church. It is impossible for Roman Catholics in one place to enter into a new relationship with another Church without involving all Roman Catholics everywhere.

Time for Coordinating Dialogues

These constitutional difficulties in the way of reunion between Roman Catholics suggest that it is now time, or will shortly be so, for Churches to conduct their conversations more widely. Roman Catholic-Anglican dialogue is now just one of many international dialogues between pairs of Churches which are being currently pursued. A few years ago, a collection of the reports of such dialogues was published, showing that joint statements had been issued by eleven pairs of Churches on a world level. The collection shows that Roman Catholics, for example, had issued statements of agreement with Lutherans, Methodists, Reformed, and Disciples of Christ, as well as Anglicans; but in fact the bilateral field has been even more fruitful than the volume indicates. Roman Catholics have been involved in dialogues with Orthodox, Old Catholics, Pentecostalists, and Non-

Chalcedonian Churches, reports of which are not included in the volume; and other agreements have been published since 1984, such as the Methodist-Roman Catholic Statement on the Church. But sooner or later, all the Churches involved in bilateral dialogues will need to come together in order to coordinate these fragmented efforts.

Faith and Order Commission

In fact, this is already being done under different auspices. The Faith and Order Commission of the World Council of Churches, which represents all the major Churches, has been working since 1927 to ascertain the extent of doctrinal agreement among them. Its greatest achievement has been the publication in 1982 of the Agreement entitled *Baptism, Eucharist and Ministry* (BEM). The 1988 Lambeth Conference, which gave such a large measure of support to the Final Report of ARCIC I, also passed a resolution recognizing "to a large extent" in BEM "the faith of the Church through the ages." The Vatican also has passed its judgment on this Statement, moving more swiftly than it has with regard to the ARCIC I Report, which still awaits Rome's verdict.

The Roman Catholic assessment of *Baptism, Eucharist and Ministry* is contained in a statement issued jointly by the Congregation for the Doctrine of the Faith and the Secretariat for Christian Unity, which bears the date of August 1987. This statement finds much to agree with in the Faith and Order document, while pointing out that it does not say all that a Roman Catholic believes it necessary to say concerning the sacraments under discussion. Despite what it sees as the incomplete nature of the document, the Vatican feels justified in affirming the contribution BEM makes to the ecumenical process.

If it were accepted by the various Churches and ecumenical communities it would bring the Churches to an important step forward in the ecumenical movement although still only one stage along the way in the ecumenical process of working toward visible unity of divided Christians. If through this process of response and reception for BEM, now being undertaken, many of the convergences, even agreements, reported by BEM were affirmed by the Churches and ecclesial communities, we believe that this would be an advance in the ecumenical movement.

Swanwick Conference

The multilateral convergence represented by BEM is evident at the national level too. A key moment in the process came in the Swanwick Inter-Church Conference of 1987 which sought a way of removing Roman Catholic objections to joining the British Council of Churches. Commentators picked out a speech by Cardinal Basil Hume as a turning-point in the Conference. "I hope," the Cardinal said,

> that our Roman Catholic delegates at this Conference will recommend to members of our Church that we move now quite deliberately from a situation of cooperation to one of commitment to each other. By "commitment to each other" I mean that we commit ourselves to praying and working together for Church unity, and to acting together, both nationally and locally, for evangelization and mission. . . . We should have in view a moving, in God's time, to full communion, or communion that is both visible and organic. . . . Roman Catholic contribution will follow from a Roman Catholic concern about the content of our faith. . . . Mission is of the essence of the life of the Church, but so is the exploration of the mystery of God. It has to be part of our dialogue arising from our common faith.

Commitment to Unity Needed

The Conference's Final Declaration showed that the Cardinal had expressed the common mind of the delegates. "It is our conviction," the statement declared,

> that, as a matter of policy at all levels and in all places, our Churches must now move from cooperation to clear commitment to each other, in search of the unity for which Christ prayed, and in common evangelism and service of the world.

Since then, the Churches in Britain and Ireland have been working at formulating a series of "ecumenical instruments," which will give permanent and practical expression to the commitment to unity which was experienced so strongly at Swanwick.

Bilateral Dialogue Still Important

These growing achievements of Faith and Order at Swanwick raise again the question whether the importance of bilateral dialogues is on the wane. Bilateral dialogues can achieve two things. They can help to remove some of the traditional disputes, suspicions, and misunderstandings between pairs of Churches in the way that ARCIC II helped to show Anglican Evangelicals that Roman Catholic teaching on justification was not as unacceptable as they had thought. Moreover, they can sometimes bring about the unity of two Churches which are already closely related, as was done in England in 1972 when the Congregational and Presbyterian Churches united to form the United Reformed Church. Bilateral dialogue between Roman Catholics and Anglicans has largely achieved the first result of discovering doctrinal agreement and removing misunderstandings. But the second aim, of uniting the two Churches, is still far short of realization; indeed, many Anglicans do not regard themselves as so close to Roman Catholics that they would want to enter into a state of communion with them if this meant excluding, say, Methodists. The Decree on Ecumenism of Vatican II stated that among the Churches of the Reformation "the Anglican Communion occupies a special place." Pope Paul VI used even warmer terms when, at the canonization of the Forty Martyrs of England and Wales in 1970, he spoke of the Anglican Church as a sister Church:

> There will be no seeking to lessen the legitimate prestige and the worthy patrimony of piety and usage proper to the Anglican Church when the Roman Catholic Church, this humble "Servant of the servants of God," is able to embrace her ever beloved Sister in the one authentic communion of the family of Christ: a communion of origin and of faith, a communion of priesthood and of rule, a communion of the Saints in the freedom and love of the Spirit of Jesus.

Sister Churches

It is evident that the references to the Anglican Communion's special place and sisterly relationship vis-à-vis the Roman Catholic Church were not intended as empty compliments but presuppose close spiritual, doctrinal, and sacramental links. It was through his contacts with the Orthodox Patriarch of Constantinople that Pope Paul learned to speak in this way of closely related Churches as "sisters." He used this term very clearly in a speech in Istanbul in 1967. The Roman Catholic and Orthodox Churches, he said, though separated for centuries were still intimately linked by the bonds of baptism, Eucharist, and priesthood in the apostolic succession:

> Now after a long period of division and reciprocal incomprehension the Lord grants us that we rediscover ourselves as sister Churches.

Differing Strategies for Unity

The passages, which accord to the Anglican Communion a special place in relation to Rome as a sister Church, suggest that in its relations with the Churches of the West, Rome would hope to achieve reunion first with Canterbury and then, together with the Anglican Communion, to seek reunion with the other Churches. We have suggested above that many Anglicans are not likely to be content with such a strategy. We must now, however regretfully, raise the question whether this strategy will remain acceptable to Roman Catholics. The "special place" which Vatican II acknowledged for Anglicans was dependent on "Catholic traditions and institutions [which] in part continue to exist" in them. Roman Catholics are bound to ask themselves, especially when they consider the implications of the ordination of women as priests, and (at the time of writing in one instance) to the episcopate, how firm is the Anglican hold on their special place. This is a painful question to ask, but, as a famous psychologist once said, "The facts are friendly." If the Anglican place among the Churches of the West is less special than it used to be, to recognize the fact will be a grace, not a confession of failure. In any event, Anglicans may be less special not only because they have in some ways moved further away from Rome but also because, as BEM has shown, the other Churches have moved closer.

Suggestions for the Future

Accordingly, perhaps the time has come for Roman Catholics to make two dramatic changes in their ecumenical strategy: to explore the possibilities of local and national rapprochement before reunion on an international level, despite the problems set out at the beginning of this chapter, and to cast more of their weight behind multilateral rather than bilateral dialogue.

This is not to suggest that ARCIC and other bilateral dialogues should forthwith cease. Not only is there still useful work for ARCIC to do on the problems set out in Chapter 6, but also the Commission has the symbolic function of expressing the two Churches' commitment to the search for unity. ARCIC II has not been relieved of the commission, entrusted to it in 1982 by the Pope and the Archbishop of Canterbury, of recommending ''what practical steps will be necessary when, on the basis of our unity in faith, we are able to proceed to the restoration of full communion.'' My point is rather that the main work of ARCIC has now been done; a way of resolving the chief doctrinal differences has been indicated. Perhaps the ''significant initiatives'' which ARCIC I called for will be taken both more widely and more narrowly than it imagined: more widely, because other Churches will be involved, and more narrowly, because the most significant initiatives may be taken at the national and local levels rather than the international. Such a shift in priorities, however, should not be viewed simply negatively, as a sign of a cooling of relations between Roman Catholics and Anglicans, but more positively as an acknowledgment of the achievement of God's grace in bringing all the Churches so close together.

In November 1980, Pope John Paul II visited Germany at a time when the people there were celebrating the 450th anniversary of that foundational document of the Reformation, the Confession of Augsburg. In a speech to the German Catholic hierarchy, the Pope urged his listeners not to allow themselves to become inured to the fact of Christian divisions. He continued:

> We often hear it said today that the ecumenical movement of the Churches is at a standstill, that after the spring of the changes brought by the Council there has followed a period of coolness. In spite of many regrettable difficulties, I cannot agree with this judgment. Unity, which comes from God, is given to us at the cross. We must not want to avoid the cross, passing to rapid attempts at harmonizing differences, excluding the question of truth. But neither must we abandon one another, and go on our separate ways, because drawing closer calls for the patient and suffering love of Christ crucified.

In his parting speech at Munich Airport, Pope John Paul had a more optimistic message:

> I hold the firm hope that the unity of Christians is already on its way in the power of the Spirit of truth and love. We know how long the times of separation and division have been. But we do not know how long the way to unity will be. But one thing we know with all the greater certainty: We have to keep on walking this way with perseverance, keep on going, and not stand still! There are many things we have to do for it; above all, we have to persevere in prayer, in an ever more powerful and intimate prayer. . . . Unity can be given only as a gift of the Lord, as the fruit of his passion and resurrection in the fullness of time appointed to it.

It is on this note that I conclude this little book.